Naughty and Nice

Naughty and Nice

◆

The Colorful Life of Transsexual Vanessa

Vanessa Mateo

iUniverse, Inc.
New York Lincoln Shanghai

Naughty and Nice
The Colorful Life of Transsexual Vanessa

iUniverse books may be ordered through booksellers or by contacting:

iUniverse
2021 Pine Lake Road, Suite 100
Lincoln, NE 68512
www.iuniverse.com
1-800-Authors (1-800-288-4677)

ISBN: 978-0-595-44624-7 (pbk)
ISBN: 978-0-595-88949-5 (ebk)

Printed in the United States of America

For my Family, Friends and the Men I love and loved

Vanessa

Contents

Introduction

While playing in the master bedroom of my grandparents' home in Manila sometime in 1980, I stumbled upon half-torn magazine pages with naked bodies of men and women. The male body—the genitalia in particular—initially caught my attention. It was the prelude to my everlasting attraction to the same sex. From then on, I became so enraptured by the male beauty.

Although outwardly I enjoyed hanging out and playing with girls when young, deep inside me rose feelings of unexplained fascination with boys my age such as crushes and other undefined feelings of admiration. Looking back, I realized that was the precursor to my homosexuality. I never had heterosexual feelings towards girls. My attraction was solely channeled on guys.

In my childhood years, I also developed an interest in many other things such as drawing, reading, and writing. I was more attuned to the academics instead of athletic pursuits. Actually, I loathed sports. Sometime in the mid-80s, I remember becoming very nervous and uncomfortable when my Daddy forced me to join the basketball team for young boys in our vicinity. I was so nervous I constantly dropped the ball from my hands or just decided to pass it most of the time during the game.

Although there were also times when I hung out with boys my age, deep inside me, I felt more comfortable with girls and girlish things. I could never exactly remember the number of friends from the opposite sex I had while growing up in the '80s. One thing I am sure of, those were some of my most happy and carefree years.

Also in my childhood years, not only was I interested in *Matchbox* toy cars, I secretly played with my sisters' and friends' Barbie dolls, too. At night, when my siblings have all gone to bed, I would sneak into our living room and play with their numerous Barbie dolls on display atop our curio cabinet. I also remember a Barbie doll of a friend that was on display inside her toy cabinet. I would always stare at it with admiration and fascination whenever I visited their house. "How pretty she is," I would say.

Throughout the years of my childhood though, I wanted to emulate girls. I remember bugging my grandmother one time, telling her I wanted to undergo surgery so I could have what Lynne (a cousin three years my junior) had "down there." This would send my grandmother to stitches. She would remind me of this brief episode with humor over and over again. I also remember asking her to send me ruffled panties during one of her overseas calls to Manila in the early '80s while she was in the US. I also recall one evening in 1984 when she and one of her nieces dressed me up in a yellow chiffon *vestida* (party dress)—a remnant of the many unsold and unused apparels she had back in the '70s when she used to own a clothing store at the town's shopping center. I clearly remember the way I swayed and turned around with glee, like the ballerina on top of a music box.

During my high school years in the Philippines, my homosexuality became more obvious but I didn't care at all. At that point, I already knew what I wanted and which sexual orientation I belonged to. Unlike other teenagers, I was not confused with my sexual orientation during my preadolescent years. I sailed onto my teenage life smoothly and walked proud and tall. I was never a weakling. I wasn't afraid nor was I ever worried.

In 1994, my family and I migrated to the US and things were completely different. Homosexuality in this country is a major societal issue, often scandalized and politicized. Whether it's one of the main courses on the political tables of the Left, Right and Conservative parties, there's always a string attached or a catch. So, why bother? Those things were the least of my worries. To me, as long as nobody messed with me and my Constitutional freedoms, the world was a happier place to live in. If ever there were some incidents of abuse or harassment, I made sure I fought back and retaliated.

These days, in this great country of ours where freedom of choice should be held sacred and respected, it is quite insulting when homosexual, lesbian and transgender students are judged by others (especially by some "conservative" and hypocritical parents and politicians) as "immorals" and "degenerates." It makes me think those "conservatives" should go back to grade school themselves and study the Constitution comprehensively.

It's funny that this issue should arise from the United States of America itself—a powerful nation whose fundamentals adhere to the respect and value for its every law-abiding citizen regardless of race, creed, religion and sexual orientation. I firmly believe that if ever this country would find itself in chaos over the issue of homosexuality, it would be the sole creation of those vituperative and hypocritical "conservatives" and their fickle-minded followers.

My entry to high school in California in the fall of 1994, up till the time I graduated two years later, seemed smooth sailing for me as a gay student. Surprisingly, the occasional teasing and taunts I experienced came not from white students, but rather from the colored ones. I was quick to put them in their proper places though. At 19, standing almost 6 feet tall, I already knew my place, and possessed a tremendous amount of maturity and courage. I knew how to show retaliation to the few bullies who harassed me.

During my brief tenure as a freshman at Foothill College in Los Altos Hills, California in the fall of 1996, discrimination against homosexuals was almost non-existent; at least in my case. At Foothill, I experienced a different kind of freedom. There were more people to become friends with, more opportunities and options for learning, and the free-to-be-you-and-me attitude was all too prevalent. I relished the brand new environment I was in.

In my early twenties, I was going through the first stages of transition from male to female. In 1999, barely a few months since my father passed away, I was androgynous-looking already. In the following year, I was living as a full-time female transsexual. I decided to welcome the new millennium with a new me.

I am now thirty years old and having a blast. I feel I have total control of my life; of things I want to experience. Someone told me that when you reach thirty you become smarter and wiser. I don't know about that. I live by the day and try to make each day meaningful and worthwhile. I know I still have a long journey in life ahead of me. First, let me push the replay button and give you a glimpse of the past thirty significant years of my life.

1

Ode to my Parents

My name is Vanessa Mateo and I am my father's son. My parents blessed me with the name 'Mark' when I was born on the 17th of May 1977, at St. Rita's Hospital in Manila.

I am the eldest of six children.

Whatever my chosen gender was, I knew very well I was loved, cared for and protected by my father. More importantly, he had always accepted me for being me. He also left an impression—his strength of character—which to this day serves as an inspiration to my daily life. Let me guide you back to his long-gone years of tests and triumphs, the dreams he had for his family, and the many advice he gave me, so that you may have a glimpse of his guiding light that continues to shine on me even to this day—a decade since his passing.

Marianito Manzano-Mateo is my father's name. He was my "Daddy." In the twenty-one years I knew him, all I ever witnessed was his determination and perseverance in giving us children a comfortable life. No matter how big the problems were, he never bowed down to defeat. My Daddy's sole goal was to safely lead us children to the right path in life, at any cost. His intelligence had no boundaries, and his common sense was quick and ever-ready, resulting in smart decisions from which we, his family, ultimately benefited. He had genuine love for his family, no doubt.

To me, he was the best father one could ever have. I know it's a cliché, an often-heard estimation coming from a child to his or her parent, but there is nothing common at all at how my Daddy ushered us to a better life.

He had to go through steels and spikes. There were constant obstacles. The years we lived in the Philippines were marked with an uncertainty in his career due to recession.

In 1987, Daddy migrated to the US. There, he strove and struggled. For seven years, Daddy was constantly away, but his love and advice were not. Although I didn't experience his guidance for a long time because of his untimely death at the age of 43 in 1998, the advice and wisdom he had instilled in me would last for a lifetime. Like what the Chesire Cat did to Alice, my father left me an indelible impression.

Daddy graduated from one of Manila's finest universities, De La Salle University. He majored in Mechanical Engineering and received his degree in 1979. By that time, he and Mommy had been together for two years, and already had two children: myself and my brother, Michael. His first job was at the assembly line company, Dynetics, and his second was with Republic Glass. The latter would be his last before he became unemployed for three straight years.

While in Dynetics in the early '80s, he would bring home *Matchbox* toy cars and cheese cupcakes for me every payday. These were my earliest recollections of Daddy's generosity; a trait which I undoubtedly inherited. Coincidentally, I believe those little toy cars helped spark my interest in automobiles from age nine; and the cheese cupcakes triggered my passion for sweets and desserts. By then, I could memorize all the models and makes the automobile companies Toyota and Ford had made locally; and to this day, my every meal wouldn't be complete without a dessert.

I'd also like to acknowledge the contribution of my great-grandmother, Leonila, to my passion and interest in toy cars. I could clearly recall her generosity in bringing me little toy cars whenever she'd visit our house. Used or brand new, it didn't matter to me. The old lady's kindness is one of the most outstanding traits I remember about her. Mommy also told me that Daddy was my great-grandmother's favorite grandson. They adored each other. She would occasionally bring Daddy some *biko* (a native dessert made with sticky rice and sweetened coconut oil) whenever she'd make it.

In 1984, Daddy lost his job with Republic Glass which resulted in feelings of depression and irritability. There were occasional arguments between him and Mommy, but I never saw him lay a hand on her. Also, by that time they had two more children: daughters Marinelli and Angeli. So, our family was growing but the income was not. It had some benefits though.

His stay-at-home position proved helpful to us children. Daddy would use his broad knowledge in mathematics and science when it came to helping me with my school projects.

I was not the smartest student in my grade school years. I didn't get perfect scores in tests nor did I receive any type of recognition; in fact, I never made it to the honor roll at all. I didn't seem to care. My interests then were playing and doing other outdoor activities—whenever I got the chance. I liked riding bicycles and playing hide and seek. Just like any other young person, I reveled in the company of friends.

During my kindergarten year, Mommy bought me a Nursery Rhymes book set. It was an epiphany. Books and reading became another preoccupation aside from childhood games. Now at 30, with dozens of books in my shelf, from King Edward VII to the Kama Sutra, I could still recite such classics as Hey Diddle, Diddle, Hickory Dickory Dock and Twinkle Twinkle Little Star; not to forget the tongue-twister Peter Piper. I am so thankful to Mommy for that great inspiration.

"Never let any stranger abuse you or take advantage of you"—another mantra I acquired from Daddy. Although he didn't utter those words directly to me, the impressions I have of him from childhood to adulthood have remained etched on my mind. It is from those memories and impressions that I derive my strength of heart and mind.

Daddy never hesitated to confront the reckless and irresponsible, especially when the lives of his children were at risk. I remember an incident sometime in 1986, while Daddy, my brother and I were crossing a busy intersection in Blumentritt, a suburb of Manila. A speeding *jeepney* (a longer version of the American Jeep used for commercial transport) driver almost hit us by a few inches; good thing the former came to his senses at the last minute and slammed on his brakes. He was too late from my father's wrath though. My father, with his almost 6 foot frame, approached the pale-faced driver and without a word threw a jab in his sorry face, yelling "You almost killed us!"

Such impressions were not limited to bad driver experiences and other situations involving the fist. When I was in fourth grade, I was involved in a minor scuffle with a fellow classmate who was bullying me. Not used to on being harassed and intimidated, I broke down at home. The teasing had something to do with my being gay. When Daddy learned about this through Mommy, he reprimanded me instead of sympathizing with me.

"I'd rather see you fighting than crying," were his unforgettable words. From that moment on, I vowed to never let anyone take advantage of me just because I preferred the company of girls in school than boys.

As the years went on, I have become stronger and more defensive. Yes, I might be effeminate to some, but that didn't mean I couldn't fight back. Bullies over the years, particularly in high school, were up to a big surprise.

In my younger years, when I was still coming to terms with my homosexuality, in the back of my mind, I also realized the world was not so accepting of individuals like myself. To make my life easier, I developed a personal shield—a stronger defense mechanism for the mind—to fight off adversity and bigotry. I realized if I would let such acts or insults affect me, I would be in bigger trouble; therefore, I should strike it down instantly, never giving it the smallest opportunity to affect an inch of my being. This strategy, along with thoughts and recollections of Daddy's unwavering courage to face life's difficulties and difficult people, have served as the solid foundation of my no-nonsense approach in dealing with prejudice and bigotry, and its instigators.

I must also point out that it wasn't just self-defense that I learned from my Daddy. He taught us children how to share, help and show compassion to others. One's strength should never be limited to physical aspects alone. A strong heart means you're ready to listen to another person's complaints and frustrations, and that you're able to give him or her advice or some form of emotional support.

My Daddy, like his father before him, had served as some sort of an unofficial *barangay captain*, or town constable, in our neighborhood. His ideas, opinions and suggestions were thought useful always. He counseled people who needed advice on certain things, and also stood as a mediator between quarreling neighbors.

In the early '90s, when he was already a US citizen, he would fly back to Manila and serve as one of the organizers of the March festivities in our area called the *Pista ng Kambal na Krus*, or the feast of the foundation of our parish church. It was his lifelong salvation. He was a devout Catholic.

He would personally pay for the traditional parish band called the *mosiko* to play right in front of our house big band style, naturally bringing entertainment to the entirety of the residents in our street who would flock near our house. He would organize native games, too, such as the *palo cebo,* where the competitors (mostly young males) would race up the top of an erected bamboo post smothered in grease; and whoever reaches the top without sliding down wins a monetary prize.

Before the dollars and Barbie dolls—when Daddy was already living and working in the US—life for us six children was a very simple one. We were not poor but not rich either.

Having five siblings and not having a lot of money during my childhood years, I learned the values of sharing, saving and sacrificing. From 1984 to the early part of 1987, Daddy was jobless. Our country's political and economical situation then—especially in the last years of the Marcos regime—was at an all-time low.

Life was a struggle. Mommy was the sole breadwinner in the family, working for the Department of Labor and Employment. She had a good job but the pay was just enough to cover our most basic needs like food and clothing.

My grandparents, thankfully, helped us with other basic needs. They provided lunch for myself and my siblings while Mommy was at work. My grandmother, Norma, also carried out the responsibility of paying for my tuition fee as well as my brother's. At the time, we were attending a private school—St. Joseph School. It was her selfless act of contribution for the betterment of my childhood. With that, I feel truly indebted and am greatly appreciative.

Daddy also helped Mommy sell cookies and Tupperware products as a *sideline* job. For their meager earnings, my siblings and I were thankful enough for the food in our table and the clothes on our back. We still felt luckier than other kids then. In the cold and cruel environs of Manila, children would roam its busy streets, begging for food or pick-pocketing just to have money to buy food.

During those "tight" times, my main concern was my siblings; that they ate well and that I took care of them well. There were days when Daddy would leave the house and go job-hunting, and no one would look after my four younger siblings except me, with the occasional help of our extended family (aunts, uncles, great-uncles). Even so, my extended family was not always available to help due to their obligations with their own families and other personal matters. My dear readers, you must remember that I was only nine or ten years old during those times—a child myself, still wanting to play with other kids, still wanting to enjoy a carefree world designed for me by fate. There were times I would peek out the window of our small house in Tondo and watch kids my age run around and play outside, wishing I was with them. I admit, I felt a little envious, but when I turned around and looked at my beautiful sisters scattered around our living room, playing with their dolls, the envy would be instantly replaced by a deep sense of responsibility.

Where I derived that sense of responsibility and maturity at such a young age, I could only guess. Maybe that's the reason why these days, I feel smarter and wiser than other people my age. I have gone through a lot, and without any tinge of regret, am very thankful for life's tough challenges in those years. If it weren't for those challenges and sacrifices, I wouldn't be the rock that I am now.

In September 1994, we finally migrated to the United States. It was an eye-opening experience, overwhelming and very exciting. I was seventeen and had seventeen thousand things going on in my mind—going to school, finding a job; basically working for a better future, and a whole lot more.

I attended two more years of high school when we arrived in the US. Daddy insisted that I earn a high school diploma here because "a high school diploma," he remarked, "would take you to places and better job positions." Again, his words were golden. In 1996, I graduated from high school, and in the ensuing years was hired by big companies like Pacific Bell, USPS and the Census Bureau.

I could still clearly recall Daddy's big, proud smile the day I graduated from high school. I knew I made him proud and conversely, I was proud to have a father who wanted nothing but the best for his child.

When Daddy died of cancer in December 1998, my world seemed darker and my burden heavier. The pressure was on. I felt like a second parent in an instant. Moments after he died, I approached my brother and four sisters and embraced them. I wanted them to know I will be there for them, too, for it would be a very tough job for Mommy to handle every thing all by herself. She would need me, and I was ready to be there for her. But first, let me tell you something about the woman who brought me into this world, for whom I am most grateful and thankful. All my precious love and deepest respect go out to her.

Hellie Naguimbing-Mateo is my mother, my "Mommy Dearest." She is a very intelligent, loving and caring woman. She is a lady who possesses the charm and beauty of a rose, and the fierce heart and determination of a warrior. From her childhood years to the death of her beloved husband, she had a life marred with challenges; but through it all, after all the storms in her life, she survived and achieved even more successes. God has been very kind to her.

Now that she's fifty, she looks back at her life with pride and a deep sense of accomplishment. She had gone through all kinds of trials and tribulations: a product of a broken family, an unwanted daughter in-law, a widow at forty-one, six children to raise and support, and an uncertain tomorrow. Nevertheless, she struggled. With her concrete faith in God serving as her armor, she faced her battles, endured and ultimately succeeded. In one of my regular *tete-a-tete* with her, Mommy would share her reflections on why God has been good to her. "Somewhere in my youth or childhood, I must have done something good," was how she would sum it up, in a Fraulein Maria style.

"Good" is a very modest estimation. Mommy was the breadwinner, not only of her immediate family, but also her relatives in the Philippines. Her kindness and generosity are perpetual. She would always lend a helping hand and offer financial support to her poor, needy relatives. She would help pay part of her nieces' tuition fees in college and send money to her sisters so they, in turn, could help their husbands sustain a family.

A Mass Communications degree holder of the University of the Philippines, it would be easy to say that Mommy seemed to have a better future drawn up for her—had she been single. Eloping with Daddy during her sophomore year in college, she already had two children by the time she graduated in 1979. She was indeed determined to finish school and have a better life. During her college years, she would juggle up parenting and studying, not to mention the dozens of household chores she had, all at the same time. "I was so skinny then and lacking sleep," she would recall. "But I struggled and carried on."

To add to her stressful life in the late '70s, there was, of course, Daddy's family. "Your grandmother didn't like me because I came from a poor family," she claimed. For Daddy, they had hoped for another daughter in-law who came from a well-to-do family, like my Uncle Mario's wife, Cynthia, who was a daughter of the vice president of La Tondena Distilleria, a major liquor company in Manila.

Mommy endured many hurtful words and scenes from my grandmother and Uncle Mario—Daddy's younger brother—one of which was when he was almost going to hit her, but didn't anyway. I had some faint visual recollections of that incident. I was only two years old, but such scene was too hard to be erased from my childhood memories. I remember a great-uncle ushering me out of the living room, so that I may not witness the mistreatment Mommy was going through—and fending off at the same time.

Although petite and skinny in frame, Mommy earned the nickname *Bunganga* (the mouth) within Daddy's family circle. For every vituperation from my grandmother and uncle, she would retaliate with an even harder sting. This is Mommy when the going gets tough. Her inner warrior comes out. Her stubbornness prevails and her bull-like temper would surely unnerve even the most formidable character she encounters.

Despite what Mommy went through though, her forgiving heart reigned. She was not the type of person who would cradle bitter feelings and grudges. Maybe that's why she's been blessed with a good, happy life. She got good karma in the end.

It also shows on her face. At fifty years old, Mommy could be mistaken for forty. She is ageless!

In the thirty years I have known her, all I have witnessed was her genuine love, care and concern, and her resilience in the midst of life's most difficult and trying moments. She is my number one and most loyal supporter. The best mother in the world and the most compassionate person I have ever known.

Her motherly love and care have continuously flourished in my heart and left a special place in my memory. I always cherish them. In my younger years, when

I couldn't sleep right away, her soothing *Lullabye* and *Tomorrow* (from *Annie*) songs calmed me and ushered me to perfect slumber.

In my adult years, when those who were prejudiced against my homosexuality attempted to bring me down and make me feel terrible, she stood in front of me to confront and scold the prime suspects. Her assertiveness, matched by an intimidating tone, surely made the culprits think twice, bowing to her formidable aura and no-nonsense approach to discrimination and other tentacles of bigotry. She made them realize they messed with the wrong mother and child duo.

One unforgettable scene that took place in 1999 was when a male sales associate at a department store in Cupertino, California taunted me for being androgynous in looks, commenting "we don't welcome people like you in our store." A brazen attack coming from an unsuspecting and misinformed individual: a department store employee whose company's lifeblood comes from the money of not only its heterosexual customers, but also those in the homosexual group.

Mommy did not hesitate to take action and ultimately confronted the store manager. The result was an apology from the latter, and an assurance of immediate disciplinary action on the part of the employee. I would have taken action myself, but decided not to; instead I let Mommy take care of it. After all, "mother knows best," and my Mommy definitely knew the best advice to give that humbled store manager, so that she may save her store from the hard knock of an imminent lawsuit.

Now that I'm 30 and am living as a full-time female transsexual, her advice and support have not wavered. My heart and mind will always be accommodating to her insights and views, to her opinions and suggestions, for I know very well they are useful and beneficial, whether today or tomorrow. Mommy is my beacon; the one person who guides me and my siblings to the right path in life—a duty Daddy likewise carried out years ago—through her sound advice, constant support and unconditional love. I am so proud and thankful to know this wonderful and incomparable human being.

2

The One and Only Vanessa

I am Vanessa, the one and only. I say this because when you go through the popular website Craigslist's *t4m* listings (transsexuals for men), there is no other name like mine.

Thankfully, there are still the nice, supportive gentlemen out there who would flag postings of other girls attempting to use my name. I tip my hat to those men because they know an extraordinary transsexual when they see one. The things I'm capable of doing, the things I have done, and the things I plan to do are solely and uniquely my own creation. They are unparalleled and absolutely original. And I am very proud of that. I'd like to welcome you to my world.

How I acquired the name 'Vanessa' was pretty simple. It was my friend Lucy's idea. Driving along busy Van Ness Avenue in San Francisco one Sunday afternoon in the spring of 2000, she blurted out (upon seeing the street sign) "Oh, so this street is called Van Ness. You should use the name 'Vanessa' then!" I thought the name was fresh and sexy, so from that point on, I assumed the name 'Vanessa'.

Before the advent of Vanessa though, there was Gemma. Lucy's friends used to call me that, particularly Rosita, the sister of Lucy's then-boyfriend, Ramoncito. Rosita was the singer/hostess for the karaoke bar Manila-Manila in Sunnyvale, California. From 1997 up until its closure in 2000, Lucy and I were frequent customers.

I never sang *in* Manila-Manila. I prefer to sing in the company of close friends or with small crowds only, especially during family parties. I just enjoyed the upbeat yet relaxing atmosphere that place offered. I also loved the food there.

To Rosita and other friends and acquaintances of Lucy, I was Gemma. I guess they named me after the tall and stately Gemma Cruz-Araneta, the Miss International beauty pageant titlist of 1964. She is Filipino. She took home the crown more than forty years ago when the ceremony was held in Long Beach, California.

Forget *Gemm*a. I'm through with it. I just want to be Vanessa. I just want to be *me*.

In this great big world with a smaller orbit of celebrities whose names start with 'Vanessa', I knew I would stand out. I admit, I am not a great actress like Vanessa Redgrave, I don't have the beauty of one-time Chanel model Vanessa Paradis nor I have the body of Vanessa Williams; but I assure you, I believe I have certain qualities that would easily attract people's attention; qualities that would create me a name of my own.

I consider myself a pre-op (pre-operation) transsexual. I am happy and content this way. In the future, I might consider breast implants, but when it comes to SRS (Sexual Reassignment Surgery) the possibility is less than zero. I will leave alone what God has *given* me. My genitalia is my priceless possession. It is a very important part of my blue print. I would hate to *lose* it.

I think this concept makes me unique in a way because I am quite sure there are many transsexuals out there who'd opt for a complete operation, to make them *totally* female. I'm very happy with what I am and have at the moment.

I also think I'm one of the few transsexuals in the world who is very happy and content with her *goodies*. I don't get stressed or go in panic mode with the fact that I don't have big breasts. From the many experiences I've had, I could very well state with a greater amount of confidence that men loved me for me, without the d cup.

I've been spoiled rotten numerous times. I've been showered with precious gifts and piles of money many times; in fact, I need another Louis Vuitton bag for my monetary possessions. It's unbelievable.

But *why*? I suppose this is an attestation that not all transsexual-loving men are after big breasts. This definitely makes me one-of-a-kind. I have that certain kind of charisma that is almost hypnotic, almost like a love potion.

Some say it's in the eyes of the charmer. I don't know about that. All I know is that men are sure to find passion and sincerity in me. I will never let them down. I'll be sure to give them the time of their lives.

I've had many fun times with the men I dated; with the *good* men, that is. There were doctors, law enforcement officers, lawyers, computer engineers, bank managers, business owners, et cetera, et cetera. You name it, I had it.

I really enjoyed all those Mercedes, Jaguar, BMW and Porsche rides my gentlemen friends gave me. I simply can not put into numbers the many times I had that kind of experience. One has to remember that even a genetic female doesn't get to enjoy these things on a regular basis, let alone another transsexual. I feel so lucky. I don't mind riding in my own Mercedes, but to me, it's more exhilirating when I *ride* in another person's Mercedes. The feeling is strangely different. Strange, yet fabulous.

I am very smart. That is the bottom line. I simply know the zigzags of dating. I know when to accelerate and take advantage, and I also know when to slow down and stop.

A friend of mine once told me I'm very lucky when it came to my dating experiences; that the men I got were the "good men." I'd say I am blessed, too, because being lucky is just a singular experience, and chances are, it won't happen to you again. I'm not lucky—rather I am blessed. Blessed with all the good things and good men this wonderful world has to offer.

Maybe my charm and sex appeal spoke for it all, along with my very positive attitude. It was all natural. I had *it* going on. I was every woman to all those men I knew. I was sweet and nurturing to them, but I also possessed a certain kind of sexual charm only found in Cleopatra and Josephine Baker.

There is only one me for sure. Like a Napoleon Bonaparte or Madonna kind of *one*. There is only one transsexual Vanessa.

3

I Do Better Things

One of the many perspectives I have in life is that God made each and every one of us uniquely special. It's all up to us if we'd let ourselves glow by showing the world those special qualities or go low and slow, ending with hardly any accomplishments in life.

I remember one pop singer whose line in one of her songs goes, "You don't have to be famous to make a difference." I think my being 5'10" tall have already made me famous—on certain websites. My admirers and supporters have repeatedly told me "there's not a whole lot of tall Filipinas around." But seriously, being famous or not famous is the least of my worries in life. My personal goal is to make a difference, set an example and ultimately create a lasting impression.

I like helping out others in need, especially my relatives in the Philippines; to remind them that I have not forgotten my roots and beginnings. I am proud to say after living in the US for almost fifteen years, never have I ignored a single letter from any relative there. As a matter of fact, there are days when all I would do is write letters and mail them the following day. That's how religious I am when it comes to correspondence with loved ones in the Philippines. I believe regular communication results in happy relationships.

I am so thankful and grateful for the care and concern those relations have shown me. Despite the fact that we're thousands of miles away from each other, they have kept in touch so devotedly, and through our correspondence, they have continuously expressed their love, support and gratitude.

In 2005, the mere two hundred dollars (equivalent to ten thousand Philippine pesos) I sent to an aunt in Manila helped her and her family open a *sari sari store*. Her litany of Thank yous and other words of appreciation was endless. She said the profits helped them cover their basic expenses, and ultimately saved them from the hard slap of poverty.

When it comes to self-representation, I want to make a difference by being polite and courteous when out in public, so that other Americans would not think some Filipinos are too abrupt or awkward in demeanor and action. I am proud to say I know how to exercise charm, charisma and deportment when in public. One doesn't have to be royalty to practice these things. Always remember, "first impressions last."

When it comes to my work-related postings and advertisements online, I do things differently. I'm proud to share with you that my posting is one of the few you'll find that does not contain lewd language and sexually explicit photographs.

There are so many other things and factors that you could associate with making a difference. Some do it in a big way, some in a small way. Oprah's humanitarian efforts were gargantuan. Her recent gift to some of Africa's children—an institution for learning—was very impressive and definitely worthy of the highest praise and recognition.

Although I don't have millions of dollars to open even a local learning institution, I know very well that the advice I give to friends and family are priceless. Through these advice they learn a lot, and eventually, they are able to apply those things to their daily life.

Once, when one of my aunts in the Philippines wrote to me, complaining about her lackluster marriage and somewhat lazy husband, I wrote back and told her "that's life for you … either you live with it or leave that guy. But then again if you leave him, what's going to happen to your children? You're a plain housewife. You don't have any employment skills. At least if you stay with him, you won't have to worry about the food on your table. At least he makes some money to cover for that."

"Practical answers for practical questions," my friend Jovette once quipped. He was absolutely right. I was able to use it when giving my distressed aunt advice.

A few weeks after I sent my response letter to that particular aunt, I received a reply from her. In it she told me that she took my advice; and that it's helping her cope with her problems and frustrations in some way.

I also had a friend who constantly needed help and advice, particularly with men and dating. Lucy, the woman who baptized me with the name 'Vanessa' was not so blessed when it came to relationships.

On one occasion in 2004, when things seemed hopeless and irreparable, Lucy was so frustrated and disillusioned that she vented "I am not a whore, where men would just dump their semen on!" It was her lowest point. It was the first time I've seen her that way.

What's a good, sincere friend to do but help another friend in need, right? I gave Lucy hope and good advice. I told her "Lucy, be very picky and try to be a little smarter. When a guy you're meeting for the first time asks you to go to your house or his house right away, use your common sense—he's no good! But if he asks you out to lunch, the movies, or to dinner, and tries to get to know you better first and *not* your bedroom capabilities, then he has good intentions and he's for keeps."

I wouldn't want my good friends *hurt*. I'd never want that to happen. So, I share them my wisdom when it comes to men and dating. I do that because I know very well I'm better at that. In general, I am good at many things.

We should also remember that making a difference starts with one's self. We have to set an example, and that's what I have been busying myself with for the past seven years of my being transsexual. I believe that in order for you to better other people's lives, you have to better yours first. Set an example. I know I'm not perfect in doing this, but rest assured I always try my very best, and fortunately, I get good results.

I've been told by a photographer friend of mine that other transsexuals he had worked with spent their earnings on signature bags, clothes and shoes. I'm not one of those; I value my hard-earned money. I would rather spend what's left of my earnings on my less fortunate relatives overseas and groceries for the household.

In the back of my mind, I know very well my massage career is only temporary. The next twenty to thirty years will take its toll on me physically. Therefore, I work hard each and every day.

I am being realistic. What better time to work more hours and start saving money than now, while I'm young and strong.

If I ever end up saving some money, I intend to go back to the Philippines and use it to start my own food business. As you can see, I have plans for a better and brighter future. I look far and wide into life. I hope others would do the same, especially the transsexuals out there.

I believe these actions I've shared with you make me stand out from the rest. I do better things than others; not just for myself, but also for people who need my help. I know very well I have made a difference; maybe not in the world stage yet, but surely amongst those who know me. It's another accomplishment in life that I am so proud of.

4

My Home

From making a difference, I would like to share with you my life at home.

In the traditional American way, a child has to move out of the house once he or she turns eighteen. I beg to differ. In my case, I would like to live here at home till I reach my eighties and nineties. This Coelho Street house is home in every sense of the word. It takes more than the adage "There's no place like home" for me to realize how important and special this edifice is. This house is no doubt home to Daddy's spirit and legacy. Every brick and stone in this house equals the every drop of blood and sweat he shelled out so that we, his six children, and Mommy, could have a house that we may proudly call 'our home'.

One day during the winter of 1996, Daddy was going through the classifieds section of the local newspaper when he surprised Mommy: he wanted to buy a house. Mommy implored him that they might not be able to afford the mortgage, let alone get approved with the loan. Little did Mommy know the significance of that abrupt decision. Eventually, they got approved with the loan and we were able to buy a house in Milpitas, California.

In less than two years, Daddy would pass away, but before it happened, he made sure his family had a house to live in, not an apartment unit where every thing was uncertain and the manager or landlord unpredictable.

Upon the purchase of our three-bedroom house in Milpitas in April 1997, the loan officer advised my parents that another member of the household must become a cosigner. Since I was the oldest child and the one with a job (my five siblings were still too young to work then), I filled in that requirement.

This did not limit to paperwork alone. During those times, the fifteen-hundred dollar a month mortgage was not easy to produce. Mother Goose certainly had better luck than us. Understandably, every one had to make additional sacrifices. Daddy never declined an overtime work offer with his job as a mail carrier; Mommy worked a second job, and I decided to work full-time, resulting in my quitting of school (I was attending college that time, aiming for a degree in History).

Through the drastic decision I made, I knew it was a major sacrifice. It was a selfless act. When other people my age were getting excited for college life, I was busying myself with cashier duties. The brighter side of it was, my family and I were able to buy and own a house.

It's been ten years since we bought this house. Time flies, but the memories linger on. There are solitary moments when I'd whisper "Thank You, Daddy, for a wonderful home." This house was his most precious gift to us.

Inside this fifty year-old abode, one would find me savoring its peace and homely appeal whenever I'm not working. It's my sanctuary; my safe haven.

Although I live with some family members which sometimes create an atmosphere of inconvenience, by the end of the day, I always look forward to coming home. I long for the comfort and warmth of my bed, and the chirping of the birds in my backyard every morning. These simple things are simply priceless.

I also revel on nights when all I'd do is eat ice cream and pizza while watching some of my favorite TV shows such as *WWE Monday Night Raw*, *The Golden Girls*, *Dirty Jobs*, *Robot Chicken* and *Anderson Cooper 360*; and of course, my favorite DVDs. What a perfect way to treat yourself after a busy, tiring day.

Some of my all-time favorite movies include *To Wong Foo Thanks For Everything, Julie Newmar*, *The Birdcage*, *The Producers*, *White Chicks*, *Clueless* and the *Pirates of the Caribbean* trilogy. No matter how many times I've seen these flicks, I'd always come back for more.

In 2006, Mommy added two bedrooms and one more bathroom, making our house a five-bedroom edifice, and automatically increasing its market value. It was a very exciting time for me.

I relished the sunny Saturday afternoon shopping trips I made with Mommy for the furniture and other accoutrements of our home. There was more space than ever, and I ultimately took advantage of it. Thanks to the many hours of hard massage work, I was able to contribute a significant amount of money to the interior and exterior renovations. It was all worth it. After all, I am sure future generations of our family would also benefit from it.

Ten years ago, while working for Walgreens and dealing with the indifference and occasional mistreatment by two of its former managers, I could very well sum up that I had good karma in the end. I remained strong and focused, and eventually survived. My hardwork, patience and perseverance paid off. Those two terrible managers might have gotten away with their atrocities but I got me a home I could very well call my own. It was an 'American dream' come true for me and my family.

As for one of those two mean managers—Mr. Maestro—a funny and interesting episode took place about five years ago (when I was already *en femme*, living as a full-time female transsexual). He responded to my Yahoo! Personals profile; he wanted to have a date with me. I'll never forget that. I saved that e-mail of his (whose address itself gave it away), along with the photo attached. Talking about what the cat dragged in!

5

Changes

After almost two years of employment with Pacific Bell as a Telephone Operator, I voluntarily resigned in March 1999 amid wrongful allegations of customer harassment and insubordination. I was indignant and determined to fight back. Surprisingly, the union leader advised me to resign to save my name and reputation because he told me I'll be fighting with the "big guys." At 22, what do I know about this union-company rigamarole. I was still grieving the loss of my father and a thousand things were going on in my mind. I eventually heeded the advice of the union leader and signed the resignation papers. He then presented me a list of possible new employers, but I was convinced it was high time that I left that line of work.

For the ensuing months after my Pacific Bell resignation I focused on helping out Mommy with parenting duties.

Due to her hectic and tiring daily schedule—juggling two jobs and a host of other responsibilities—I played the role of housekeeper and chauffeur. In the morning, I would drop off my three younger sisters to school and pick them up in the afternoon. In between, I would perform a succession of household chores. I also made sure I brought the girls to their doctor and dentist appointments. I never complained. A sense of devotion to my family and concern for their well-being were the major factors that drove me to do it. I knew very well no one would perform those tasks but me.

To give myself some diversion from a hectic family life, I took classes at Foothill College in Los Altos Hills, California, where three years prior I entered as a freshman. Naturally fond of music and people, I enrolled for classes in Music and Psychology. With the former course, I was able to familiarize myself with classic arias and their composers. It was my temporary therapy from the ever busy life I was living.

But something deep inside of me wanted to burst out. I knew it was something very significant. I knew it would benefit me and bring me more happiness.

I wanted to become a full-time female transsexual. I had this revelation a long time ago.

Living as a woman was a long-overdue plan. I knew it would be a great fulfillment. I've been dreaming about it for years. When I was young, I knew already I was gay, but as I grew older, my homosexuality was leaning towards the path of becoming a female transsexual. It wasn't just a strong feeling of femininity though; it was an urge to completely live as a woman.

The desire to live as a woman started in 1998, while Daddy was still alive. Deep inside me, I knew I possessed the heart of a woman. It has been commonly noted that female transsexuals are "women trapped in a man's body." I truly believe that.

Having the guts and nerve to transform myself from male to female was a major challenge. I asked myself a thousand times how my friends and family would take it. Will they accept me or hate me? Regardless, I went on with it. I realized if they really loved me, no amount of hair and make up should change that fact.

By the middle part of 1998, I started growing my hair longer and experimented with make up. When out in public, I definitely looked androgynous. I recall a somewhat embarrassing encounter at the In-N-Out burger joint in Sunnyvale, California, when a young guy approached me and politely asked "Are you a guy or a girl?" My simple and short response was, "I'm like you."

Comments about my androgynous looks weren't limited outside the house at all. Once, when Daddy was still alive and we were having a family dinner at home, he jokingly asked why my eyebrows were thinning; that when I was born I *had* eyebrows. He also made comments about my lips being red (because of lipstick), but they weren't insulting in nature nor he intended to do so in the first place.

My Daddy, after all the changes and decisions I made in life while he was around, never said a hurtful or degrading word. He was all fatherly business; giving advice instead of attacking my sexual orientation; letting me become what I wanted to be instead of leading me towards his plans and ambitions like what some fathers would do to their sons; and constantly serving as the pillar of the family, ever ready to protect and support his children in every possible way, whether they're gay or straight.

By the latter part of 1999, almost a year after Daddy passed away, my gender transition was well underway. From the very beginning of this journey, I knew very well it wouldn't be just about the change of physical appearance. There were many major changes involved. It would also consist of making my demeanor more feminine and graceful, changes in attitude and ultimately my lifestyle.

I struggled with the change and transition process. I was so clueless about what clothes to wear. I was left in the dark when it came to the kinds and shades of make up to use on my face.

My main goal was to look passable without undergoing any kind of surgery, so I started experimenting with make up and women's clothing. I have repeatedly tried different bra designs and sizes, different shades of make up, and different hairstyles which would hopefully make me look more feminine.

I somehow managed to look passable though: employees at Foothill College addressed me as "ma'am" on two separate occasions. But I looked matronly. I was not the petite type. At 180 pounds, towering at 5'10", I definitely looked mature. Also, I was into dark-colored fabrics and red lipstick. Not good. These dark and strong shades did nothing but highlight the masculinity of my face. I still felt uncomfortable.

Over time though, I got over my worries and frustrations. I paced myself into steady and uninterrupted development. I resigned myself with the fact that I only had two choices: make it or break it. Somehow I managed to survive and live with it.

In December 1999, I was hired by the United States Postal Service in San Jose, California for their seasonal employment program. I worked the graveyard shift. I enjoyed the company of other employees there, regular or temporary. The night shift manager, Marlyn Foxworthy, even offered me to come back for the month of January. I got along well with many of them; until one night when I decided to use the women's restroom.

Before I share with you what happened, let me first tell you about another incident that took place outside the men's restroom. I was on my way there when another male employee prevented me. He yelled "Hey, you're in the wrong place!" Embarrassed, I uttered "I'm sorry" in the best female voice I could, almost to a whisper register. I walked away afterwards.

I knew some male employees there (especially the non-Filipino) took me as a female. They didn't have the slightest idea that I was male. I suppose my efforts in attempting to look like female was paying off. But I also had to pay the consequences.

Filipinos, in contrast to other nationalities, are most discerning when it comes to gender. They could easily identify the true gender of an individual, regardless of how hard the other party tries to look feminine *or* masculine. This stems from the notion that in the Philippines, transsexuals are old news. *We* have always been part of the society even though not all people in my country are accepting and open-minded.

Just because one lives in a tolerant country like the United States does not mean a Filipino I'd meet here would be tolerant as well with my sexual orientation. Either he or she hates me or accepts me; it's as simple as that.

Now, back to my little post office episode. As I entered the women's restroom, some Filipino women present gave me the look. I even overheard one of them blurted out "What's he doing here?" Fortunately, I knew who she was. It was also confirmed by one of my friends present at the time. When I got out of the stall, she pinpointed the person who made that remark (but I already recognized who the culprit was through her distinct, arrogant tone of voice though).

From the very beginning of my employment at that USPS office, I felt a certain kind of indifference from her. She wasn't the friendly type. Once I smiled at her, she just stared back at me like a statue. Her tattooed and arched eyebrows gave way to her discriminatory nature: they were always raised, like Morticia Addams'. I could tell she had some bigotry in her veins. I am not stupid. I know hatred when it surrounds me. I am *that* smart.

The following night, upon arriving at work, I was summoned by the supervisor. He was a balding, middle-aged Filipino guy. He reprimanded me for using the women's restroom. Apparently, Miss Mean Eyebrows made a complaint. But she obviously underestimated my capabilities and retaliatory tactics. Both of them were up to a big surprise.

The following night, I counterattacked. This time, I spoke with a non-Filipino supervisor. Mr. X was a big and tall white guy whom I felt comfortable filing a complaint to. I knew very well that a non-Filipino supervisor would take my sentiments seriously, and not dismiss it like something of a minor rift.

As I began my shift that night, I approached the friendly gentleman and asked if I could speak with him about an important matter. He obliged, set aside what he was doing at the moment and listened to my complaint.

So, I recounted the events—in a very thorough fashion. I went through every detail, from date to time. Mr. X just listened. I told him "I was a victim of sexual discrimination and harassment, and you have to do something about it." From that very moment, Mr. X assured me that he will take care of it, and that I may use the women's restroom without any worries or hesitation at any time.

Sure enough, I did just that. For the following nights and throughout the remaining days of my employment at that USPS branch, not one person fretted against my right to use the women's restroom; let alone get another reprimand from the biased Filipino supervisor. As for Miss Mean Eyebrows, she could raise her eyebrows all she wants, but one thing I am sure of, I won and had the last laugh.

The USPS skirmish was a blessing in disguise. It shot up my confidence level to an all-time high. I realized I could fight back when it came to my basic rights and privileges as a transgender; that I am fully entitled to the benefits and freedoms offered by any institution or establishment to their employees regardless of my sexual orientation. I also discovered that one has to really speak out and be heard, and not stop until a problem is solved or an issue resolved. Lastly, I simply have to use the women's restroom always; that no amount of eyebrow raising and unsolicited comments would deter me from doing so.

Wherever Mr. X is now, I'll never forget him. I am very thankful and grateful for his help. He was one of those few supervisors in existence who knew how to show genuine concern for the rights and basic privileges of their employees. He also did something very important for me: he opened the door for more changes.

6

Turmoil

In late 1999, one year after Daddy's passing, I still felt depressed in some way. I was confused, too. "Is becoming a woman what I really want?" I asked myself. It was like having a circus going on in my head—too many circles, too many turns. I didn't know where to go.

My Mommy and I had some sporadic arguments over this matter. Maybe at first she assumed I was only experimenting; that the tide would turn and I'd go back to looking straight, and not dress as a woman anymore.

I wouldn't blame her. At the time, she was still grieving the loss of her beloved husband and dealing with a host of problems and challenges such as raising four younger children, financial matters and harassment by some of Daddy's relatives (who wanted part of his insurance policy). For me to add up to the truckload of problems was too much for her.

The one and only time she confronted me about my transition from male to female came in early 2000, when I was on my way to the Newpark Mall in Newark, California. She became a little upset upon seeing me in a lavender blouse with plunging neckline and full make up on. After that incident, we didn't speak for a couple of days. Finally, on the third day, she initiated a conversation and we embraced each other afterwards. She told me "I just didn't want you to get hurt." After that incident, I felt she had accepted the fact that living as a woman was my chosen path.

Although my family loved me unconditionally and open-heartedly, I was yearning for a different kind of love and appreciation. Alongside the feelings and urges to live my life as a woman was the desire to be with men. What better validation to get than to be with a man, right? "After all," I told myself, "a man would nicely complement a woman … that's life." I was wrong.

In 2000, the new millennium was ushered in and I felt a new kind of ecstasy. "Celebrate the new millennium with a bang!" I told myself. I wanted to get out there and party, be merry, and have a blast. For a moment, I didn't care much about those troubling emotions I felt. I thought that if I hung out with new friends, particularly with men, my attention would be diverted.

At the same time, my looks were improving. My hair had gotten significantly longer, and with the help of my cousin's Mexican wife, Juliana, my wardrobe and choice of clothing in general had improved as well. Juliana handed me the mini skirts, high heels and low-cut blouses she quit wearing months prior due to her pregnancy. It worked out perfectly because our body sizes were almost the same—bordering around 12 and 14.

With my looks improving and I'm looking more feminine, men followed suit. All of a sudden, I was being bombarded with e-mails from curious Johns and Georges, asking for dates and several rendezvous. I became excited and felt flattered. "Wow! They all want to date me!" I told myself. The thought of possible lunch, dinner and movie dates lifted my spirits and took me to a higher high. Also, I was looking forward to exhibiting my sexy, new clothes in public.

In reality though, those men were so embarrassed to be seen in public with me that they preferred we just stayed in their cars and trucks. There were a few who took me out to dinner and lunch dates; some were even more daring to take me to the movies.

But the majority just wanted a *private* time with me.

I was in my early twenties and my sexual libido was sky-high. I obliged with the sex and other carnal activities. To me, it was a two-way street. But most of the time I didn't get any satisfaction. The men I dated back then were the selfish type.

I sometimes felt awkward being with them because they made me feel that way in the first place. They drained the positive energy I had. They brought in negativity and showed negative attitude.

I became so disillusioned. I was very disappointed, too. What I previously thought would be a celebratory time in my life then turned out to be completely the opposite.

Aside from the "car dates" I had with those men, strangers' homes and hotel rooms were the only places I had fun at, and they were obviously temporary. At the end of the day, I was alone again. Sometimes I would drive home late at night, feeling used and abused. Still, because of my being young, curious and libidinous, I did not hesitate to satisfy my craving for sex. I didn't seem to mind the drawbacks caused by the activities which I involved myself in.

I reveled in the company of young men though. They offered some kind of consolation. With their fresh approach to life and positive energy, they gave me temporary relief from the disappointment and disillusionment I felt. Strangely enough, although I knew they were after the sex too, they made me happy and gave me hope.

Through the regular e-mails and occasional phone calls I received from my young bedroom companions, I had something good and long-lasting to look forward to: better treatment.

7

So Many Men, So Many Experiences

Boytoys

First on my roster of young lovers was this white guy from Gilroy, California whom I would regularly meet for fun in the early years of my being *en femme*. Ross Wills was his name—a very good-looking eighteen year-old with a passion for motorcycles, big trucks and transsexuals.

I first met Ross in May 2000. He responded to my Yahoo! Personals profile and had expressed his sincerity to meet. He was the first young white guy I dated; therefore, it was a very memorable experience.

Berryessa Road (in San Jose) would be our favorite hotspot, whether it be at the Dennys restaurant parking lot, some isolated spot off Baton Rouge Street, the Safeway parking lot or somewhere along Mabury Street.

Ross was very nice to me, but like any other testosterone-loaded teenager, he was just not ready to commit to a serious, faithful relationship, let alone be with a transsexual. I respected that. Back then, my estimation on teenage guys and other young men was not complicated at all: they were only good for quickies.

His beauty, body and bedroom performance were more than enough for me to keep him on my top ten list for many years to come. A gym buff with tattoos, and possessing gorgeous hazel eyes, I was constantly under his spell. Being a Taurean, beauty is my greatest weakness. I might be a bull in other aspects of life, especially on being stubborn when it comes to making final decisions, but in the presence of beauty, I am disarmed. I would bow down to my master in an instant.

Ross provoked me in many different, sexy ways. More importantly, he made me feel like a woman whenever we were together. In some unusual way, I felt I belonged to him like a girlfriend, and him to me as a boyfriend.

In all fairness, Ross had very good qualities, too; not just with matters concerning his bedroom performance. At a young age, he already displayed gentleman qualities. Once, when we stayed at the Days Inn hotel on Tully Road in South San Jose in August 2003, he made sure he handed me a glass of wine first before he gulped down his own drink. Some young men wouldn't even dare buy you a bottle of water in the first place.

Ross have kept in touch with me over the years. It's hard to believe that it's been seven years since we first met. We were both young and unsure of what we were going to do; of who would make the first move; and what would be the outcome of that meeting—whether or not he'd still want to see me after or erase me from his memory as quickly as he drove away in his lifted white Dodge pick up truck.

With Ross, it has been a good and meaningful relationship. I don't look at him as a *boytoy* of some sort, or a 'friend with benefits', rather he serves as a reminder that there are still respectful young men out there who, despite being one step short of treating me like a real girlfriend, still possess the genuine warmth of a caring individual.

In an e-mail he sent me in early 2007, Ross stated that he had hoped sex was "not the only factor" why our relationship lasted for seven years. Whatever he meant by that or however he wanted me to respond to that, I'm content with the fact that our friendship is still alive, and remains special in some way.

In April 2000, one month before I met Ross, I met another good-looking young man by the name of Josh. He was my very first Latin *papi*. Like Ross, he also responded to my Yahoo! Personals profile. Josh lived in Petaluma, California. We met a couple of times—in 2000 and 2001; the location being the Golden Gate area of San Francisco. I could clearly remember that beautiful starlit spring night we first met; he took me for a short walk along Vista Point, holding my hand, and drove me by the shores of the Marin Headlands wherein he showed me a different kind of heaven. His white Honda Civic was completely fogged out; and as a gesture of satisfaction, I drew "A+" using my index finger on the passenger side window.

I never saw Josh again after our May 2001 meeting. The last time we came into contact with each other was in early 2006, when he responded to my Casual Encounters posting on Craigslist. We made indefinite plans to meet, but it never materialized.

I'm content on leaving things that way. When I look back at our trysts, I simply close my eyes and relive the sweetness of his kisses and the smoothness of his toned, alabaster-white thighs. The exciting memories of those two encounters are enough to keep my two dozen winters warm.

Brian Maybird was another young man who caught my keen eye, and eventually became one of my most favorite *loverboys*. Nineteen at the time when I first met him in January 2001, he was a Chico State student with a James Dean appeal—square jaw, dark blond hair and Hanes-clad. He responded to my Yahoo! Personals profile and we agreed to meet at a hotel in Fremont—the Good Nite Inn by Cushing Parkway. At the time of our meeting, it was his college's winter break and so he was back in town to spend some time with his family and fortuitously, with me.

I was so turned on upon seeing him because he had that certain sex appeal which was indescribable. He was very good-looking, too. I have a penchant for referring to young men as "fresh meat," and for me, Brian was comparable to a freshly cooked turkey: tender and mouth-watering. I was salivating and ready to *consume* him.

In bed I gave him the "standard pleasuring" I normally give my lover within the first few minutes of intimacy. I didn't let the flames of passion envelope me just yet. I started by slowly teasing him and ended up getting wild on him. I was on top of Brian. He enjoyed it a great deal, so great that after a few minutes of penetration and kissing he muttered "Oh Vanessa, I think I came already."

After our first encounter, it would be a little over a year before we'd see each other again. Sometime in March 2002, he sent me an e-mail telling me he was back in town and that we should meet again. He indicated in his e-mail that he had come back to the Bay Area to finish his college studies and decided to complete his credits at a local community college instead of Chico State.

When we met that March, we decided to get a room at the same hotel. This time, Brian had grown and improved, physically. He had a more muscular, toned build and was exuding control and confidence which aroused me even more. Nothing like being "dominated" by a younger man. It was a complete turn on for me, because instinctively, I knew from the very beginning I had a strong personality, and so to become submissive to another—particularly inside the bedroom—sparked a curiosity. I wanted to know how it would turn out. This time, I was ready to submit to Brian's sexual demands and orders. The fact that he was younger than me made the situation even more exciting and erotic.

During our intimacy, I let Brian took control of me and my senses. I wanted to know if he was ready to dominate me, automatically confirming the master-like demeanor he had been showing. This time, Brian was on top of me, talking dirty to me and making love to me uncontrollably. It was our best meeting so far.

It dawned on me that after that meeting, Brian was no *boytoy* anymore. He was starting to learn the ropes of becoming a sexually-aggressive man. I still enjoyed our time together though.

Our last meeting was in April 2003. I rented a room at a hotel along Mission Boulevard, also in Fremont. During that encounter, Brian became more aggressive and dominant. The verbal abuse was like Mozart playing in my ear. I was so looking forward to the intensity of its outcome. Sure enough, the flawless crescendo of the orgasm caused by it was intense. Never before a younger man had given me such total satisfaction. It put Brian on my "elite list" of *boytoys*.

But just like a good song, there is an end to it. It was the last time I saw Brian. I think I have an answer to this. In an e-mail he sent me before our last meeting, he mentioned he had an overly protective—to the point of nagging—girlfriend; that he wouldn't be able to meet me in the evening anymore, and that our time together would be curtailed.

Obviously, he was afraid of being caught or being suspected of cheating. I was totally aware of such drawbacks and barriers in a regular man-woman relationship.

Men, being the formidable creatures that they are, naturally frown upon the idea of having limits and restrictions set upon them. It is ironic and unfortunate how they fall victim to their conniving, scheming, jealous and insecure wives and girlfriends. I feel a tremendous amount of pity for those men who are in this category. Hopefully they'd remain single; that they do not commit to a serious relationship unless they know in their hearts that the woman they're with is the *one*.

Coming from the northern part of the Bay Area is Sam Chacon, another nineteen year-old I met in 2002. This handsome Latin *loverboy* was definitely infatuated with transsexuals from the very beginning, and I was no exception to the roster of "trannies" he had fantasized of being with.

Like Ross and Brian, we met through Yahoo!. We didn't meet right away, rather we chatted over the phone and exchanged e-mails first. In the spring of 2002, he drove some 50 miles to Milpitas and met me at the McDonald's restaurant not far from my house. He was driving a black nineties' model Chevy Impala at the time. The car stood out because I could clearly remember being seated so comfortably on its passenger side. Chevrolet cars and trucks are some of the most spacious you could find.

A few weeks after that first meeting, we agreed to rendezvous in Novato, California where he rented a room at the Days Inn. In there, for the very first time, I had my first time with Sam. His *style* was very typical of a teenager: wham-bam-thank you-ma'am. I didn't complain. Why would I? I was having a blast in the company of an energetic young man. Sam gave me that certain kind of excitement in the bedroom that I had been missing.

In January 2003, I embarked on a disastrous relationship with a man thirty years my senior. It was a short episode in my life which I prefer not looking back to, although my sexual relations with Sam had something to do with his house: we did the "dirty deed" there.

The best and most kinky fun I had with Sam was at the house of my then-boyfriend, Ronald Hubert of San Leandro, California. Not only it was the most fun, but it was the funniest experience as well. It was a one-time experience that served as an anathema to the dull and disillusioning relationship I had with Ronald.

From January to May 2003, I was in a committed relationship with Ronald. Twice a week (once during the week and another on a Saturday or Sunday) I would stay at his house and spend the night there.

One day in April, I invited Sam over. It was around three o'clock in the afternoon. Ronald would arrive home around five or a little after. So, Sam and I had roughly about two hours to get intimate. We decided to do *it* in the living room so that if something unexpected happens (for example, Ronald arrives home earlier than normal, or his neighbor comes knocking at the door for some reason) we would be warned immediately.

While Sam and I were having intercourse on the couch by the living room window, I heard a sound of what seemed to be a pick up truck with monster exhaust pipes parking outside. I then took a peek—while Sam was still *inside* me. It was a *Desperate Housewives* moment for me. Strangely enough, I was loving every second of it. I like taking risks sometimes.

Coincidentally, Ronald's son, Ron Jr., who was living in Virginia at the time, had a similar pick up truck. In my panic and utter shock though, it didn't occur to me that Ron Jr. was thousands of miles away from San Leandro. To make the situation more frightful, the guy driving the pick up truck had shaved head—completely resembling that of Ronald's son.

Thinking of the worst outcome—being caught, above all—I hastily broke away from Sam, and promptly instructed him to put his clothes back on and leave through the backdoor. I was in panic mode at its highest level.

Fortunately for both of us, the guy driving the pick up truck started talking to the next door neighbor, and eventually entered the latter's house. It was both a confirmation that it was not Ron Jr., and that every thing was false alarm. As Sam walked towards the backdoor, I summoned him back, informing him that everything was false alarm. I then instructed him to resume what he was *doing* before.

To be very honest, I almost had a heart attack. If it ever really was Ronald's son, and he caught me with another man—inside his father's house—the scene would be absolutely chaotic.

It's been over three years since it happened, and whenever I reminisce that episode, I somehow find it amusing.

In the fall of 2003, Sam moved to Los Angeles to attend college, and so our meetings ended. From time to time though, he would send text messages asking me when I would drive down to Southern California so we could meet. For some reason, the idea was not appealing to me anymore because in my mind, LA should only remind me of the one special boy who, for one night only, made me feel like the most beautiful and most captivating girl on earth—the envy of all women and the desire of all men. This I will explain and elaborate later.

Coinciding with my sexual relationships with Brian and Sam was that with a young and handsome Portuguese-American guy named Kyle Binetts. Twenty-two years old when I met him in the fall of 2001, with a tall, lanky build and possessing dark, good looks, I was instantly smitten.

Kyle seemed like a mystery waiting to be unraveled—at least that's how I fancied him at the beginning of every meeting we had. At first, he would seem quiet and shy, but once we start doing intimate things, he would gradually become aggressive and dominant.

As our "session" progressed, Kyle emerged as a skilled and willing lover. Despite his youth, he made sure I was pleased and satisfied first. This aspect would prove significant in my relationships with the three: Brian, Sam and Kyle. It's the attitude that sets them apart from their slightly older counterparts (those men whose age ranged from twenty-four to twenty-seven). I felt lucky to have met such giving and patient lovers.

Kyle and I would meet at the Hot Tropics Spas in San Lorenzo, California. He used to drive a maroon '80s Chevy pick up truck with loud exhaust pipes. The noise would serve as the warning announcement of his arrival at the parking lot. We would then walk inside, rent a spa room for an hour, and have our fun.

Kyle enjoyed sensuality the most. He loved the massages I gave him while he was half-soaked in the spa. After a few minutes in the pool, we would settle ourselves on top of the cushioned bench and make love.

Kyle would always satisfy me to my heart's content. He made sure I had my orgasm. Only after I *released* would he then ask for his own.

The last time I saw Kyle was in late 2002. The following year he married. Although we would continue to communicate through the internet for another few months, and even made plans for another meeting, it never materialized.

Kyle seemed caught between a mental tug-of-war of being devoted to his wife and the desire to see me; in the end the former won.

In late 2006, Kyle called me up just to say hello and see how things were going with me. It was a total surprise. It brought a smile to my face, of course. Even though I don't see these so-called *boytoys* in person anymore and get intimate with them, the memories of the fun and pleasure I had with them would forever stay on my mind. I just wish them the best and hope that they'll find true happiness in the new adventures they've embarked on.

Not all the young men I met in the early years of my *womanhood* abandoned me. There were the good, loyal ones, too.

One of those good, loyal ones was Derek Norton of Fair Oaks, California. Twenty-two years old when I met him in the summer of 2001, Derek was just too nice to a fault. He was one of the most courteous, respectful and humble guys I ever met. Like Ross and Josh, he responded to my Yahoo! Personals profile, and we eventually clicked. He was 6 feet tall, with an athletic build and very expressive light brown eyes. He once told me he was of Scottish descent. I didn't doubt that at all, because for some odd reason, his side-view profile had a striking resemblance to that of the Marquess of Lorne, the Scottish-born son in-law of England's Queen Victoria. Although not altogether handsome, Derek had that strong, masculine appeal which was quite a turn on for me.

Our dates regularly took place in Hayward, California. Derek used to work as a delivery man for a warehouse company along Industrial Parkway, and whenever he would be in town, he would call me up and we would meet. He would arrive around midnight, drop off packages, and when he was done, we would meet at the nearby Dennys and get a room at the Motel 6 right next to it.

Derek was crazy mad over my pleasing skills. I could tell because if you know you are doing a good *job,* you could feel it through the throbbing of your partner's penis, or with the way he moans and catches his breath—as if he is having a heart attack.

With the physical aspect of our relationship—the sex part—everything seemed fine. Emotionally, I knew we both suffered from a dilemma: I couldn't give him the pleasure of penetrating a vagina, and he couldn't give me one hundred percent sexual satisfaction by making me reach orgasm. This stemmed from the fact that he had not the slightest idea that I was a transsexual.

For some odd reason, Derek did not have the common sense to figure it out through my deep voice. He had always thought my voice was "sexy," and constantly referred to me as the "sexy lady." When there were times we couldn't be with each other physically, we would resort to phone sex. Derek would easily reach orgasm with all the "exciting" things I'd tell him over the phone.

Our friendship bloomed as the months and years went on. We dated from August 2001 until February 2004. Derek didn't have a lot of money, but that didn't change our friendship a bit. In fact, I would occasionally help him with gas money; considering the fact that he would drive about one hundred miles just to see me. I would grant him this simple act of generosity whenever he would use his own car, not the company van. For someone to go through that trouble just to be with me even for a short period of time means a lot, and I simply have to do them justice. I know some people might think of it as unconventional (especially in my culture, wherein if a woman gives money or other material things to her lover or boyfriend, she is instantly judged as a walking piggy bank), but I hardly cared. Mine was a simple act of appreciation.

Derek came from a middle-class family in Northern California. He lived with his homemaker mother and an invalid stepfather. He had an older brother in New York whom he would visit from time to time. Where they got the financial means to survive, I never asked. My main concern was our friendship and the burning question "Does he know?"

Derek never asked me about my true gender. He was just the typical all-American guy who loved sports, beer, having a good time and women. Yes, he had genetic female friends, too. He would talk about them occasionally—snippets of their lives, his friendship with them and other things. Regardless, I was never jealous about these things, for I knew deep inside I could never give him what those other female friends could—if ever he became intimate with any of them. I had the put-up-or-shut-up attitude towards it.

I contented myself with hopes that maybe—and hopefully—Derek prioritized me first. It was like letting a pigeon fly free; if it comes back then you know his loyalty is with you.

Despite our carefree and happy relationship, I was still worried about the consequences once he realized that I was born male. Such revelation would be very harmful to our friendship.

Regardless, my dates with Derek continued. For the many times I gave him all the pleasures he craved for, the many times he repeatedly asked me if he could return the favor. He wanted my "pussy"—a thing I didn't have.

When 2004 rang in, our dates became less. By the middle of that year, it became non-existent. The last time I heard from him was in May of that year. I was surprised when he sent me a text message on my cell phone, asking me when I would be able to meet again. Previously, there was a gap in our relationship.

During the three-month period (from February to April) that I didn't hear from him, I figured he became seriously involved with one of his other female friends.

I was just too instinctively smart not to figure that out. Not hearing from him even for a week was unbecoming of Derek; at least he would call twice a week. So why the three months gap then?

During those times, I was also busy with my studies. I went back to college briefly to attend Massage Therapy classes at the De Anza College in Cupertino, California. It kept me preoccupied, and my hectic schedule prevented me from other activities, especially meeting with someone late at night when I knew I had to get up early for school the next morning. I simply had to use common sense for that matter.

Whether or not Derek eventually discovered my true gender remains a question which I would not worry about anymore. I closed that chapter with him in my life with a clear conscience and firm mind set that we both had fun and we both benefited from it.

In early 2007, he started communicating with me again. In one of the numerous text messages he sent me, he gave me an update about his current status: separated from his wife and already a father of a two year-old girl. He is currently going through court proceedings—he wants a divorce. I wasn't surprised or shocked anymore, because three years ago, I had a gut feeling he entered a serious relationship with someone. I was right.

When I hear things like these I feel sorry for the men, and look up to their misfortunes with a tinge of humor. They are so imbued with the delights and pleasures brought by their carnal conquests that they underestimate the consequences. I wish they had exercised some common sense.

In addition to seeing these young men, with what was left of my spare time, I managed to rendezvous with other men. This time around, the guys were professionals; more experienced and fully aware of what they wanted to have and do.

These men were decent and accommodating enough to invite me to their houses and apartments. They happened to be single men who needed a "girl-friend experience"—with kissing, hugging, and petting—or in other words, have those romantic aspects found in a genuine, committed relationship minus eating out at restaurants or going to the movies. I didn't care. My main goal was to get pleasure and give pleasure. I was in my mid-twenties, and my sexual libido was at its highest peak. I was like a brand new Ferrari ready to be revved up, ridden and driven.

I never had so much pleasure from giving pleasure in my sexually-charged transsexual life than with these two good-looking, semi-mature men: Carl Heastrom and Mike Best. Coincidentally, their houses were not far from each other—located right along Union Avenue in San Jose. Although they didn't know each other personally, one thing they had in common was pleasing me in the bedroom, and making me very happy.

I met Carl and Mike in 2001 and 2002, respectively, and I must admit those years were some of the most sexually exciting and gratifying for me. Even though we would not meet regularly, as opposed to my trysts with my *boytoys*, there seemed to have been some kind of loyalty in the air between myself and these two men.

Blue-eyed Carl and I first met in September 2001. Just like his numerous *forebears*, he responded to my Yahoo! Personals profile. He used to live at a condominium complex along Snell Street in San Jose, and later moved on to a house by Union Avenue.

How could I forget that condominium complex? One balmy summer night in 2002, while on my way to see Carl, I was pulled over by two police officers (as part of their "routine traffic stop" work), reprimanded me for having a suspended driver's license, and to my surprise, let me go with just a warning. I was definitely luckier than Paris Hilton. I suppose my charming personality, paired by an aquamarine halter top and white denim shorts, were enough to make them reconsider.

Now, back to Carl. He was most accommodating. I remember the first time we met, he made me feel really comfortable as if we had known each other for years. He welcomed me to his home like a friend, not as a stranger. After a short conversation, he then served me wine and later offered his sexy, muscular body.

In bed, he was also very welcoming. Carl definitely enjoyed my creativity. Carl enjoyed having his whole body pleased and caressed, and I did so in many different, stimulating ways. I was at the peak of my being kinky, and in my mind, the possibilities were endless. I was most happy to give him that kind of pleasure, because in the deepest and darkest realms of my mind, I loved doing it anyway. It pleased both my body and senses. It was a two-way street kind of pleasure.

One binding principle I have in the bedroom is that whatever I find sexually arousing and satisfying, I would go for it, regardless how nasty or taboo.

Though not blessed generously in height, Carl made it up through his generous behind. It was round and firm, and had a protruding profile. For a butt-admiring person like myself, it was absolutely arousing. I thought I had hit jackpot every time we hit the bedroom.

At the time, Carl was living with a roommate; a roommate who "doesn't appreciate" girls like myself. So, our meetings were limited. We'd meet only when the roommate was not home.

Working for a company that sends its people out of town constantly proved to be a minor barrier for my meetings with Carl. Regardless, I was most happy and satisfied whenever we were together. The fact that this handsome gentleman was confident and trusting enough to have me over—a transsexual he didn't know very well—was a very nice act. It makes me shout out to the criticizing world that I am respected and appreciated, and to top it all, am having a blast with one of America's most good-looking men.

Sex with Carl was a combination of passionate and kinky. He took his time. His style of lovemaking was representative of a semi-mature man in his early thirties just beginning to master the art of sex, with all the romantic aspects. To enhance the romantic atmosphere that was starting to get intense by the minute, Carl would light up aromatic candles, adding to the fragrance I'm already enjoying—emanating from his freshly-showered body.

Carl was not the two-minute kind of lover I found in other men, especially those in their teens and twenties. When those young studs would ride their girlfriend fast as if they were competing at the Kentucky Derby, Carl would give it to me gently with sweet concern. Periodically, he would ask me questions such as "Are you ok?" or "Am I going too fast?"

Carl was also a master when it came to helping me reach orgasm. The image of his healthy butt cheeks near my face only enhanced the very erotic and kinky atmosphere that had already been permeating his bedroom. Occasionally, he would talk dirty to me because Carl knew all too well it would only intensify the lust that had been dominating my veins.

I am so aroused by the psychological aspect of sex. Whenever I reach the apex of my orgasm, I totally lose control. It's truly "heaven on earth."

Unbeknownst to Carl, another lover with a very loveable behind—Mike Best—was residing not too far from where he lived. Mike, like many of his *predecessors*, responded to my Yahoo! Personals profile in the fall of 2003.

Our first meeting was memorable because he was accommodating enough to even cook me dinner—grilled chicken breasts with steamed vegetables and red wine—and let me stay the night. No other man had done that for me in previous years. Mike left a very good impression.

What set Mike apart from the other men I met was his incomparable confidence and self-assurance, especially during situations which to some might seem completely impossible to turn into reality in the first place. The fact that it was our first time together and that he decided to bring me with him to Kmart in San Jose—a very public, crowded place—was a very brave and praiseworthy act. He disregarded and ignored possible criticisms which might have been triggered by the sole fact that I was a transsexual. Mike was confident enough to parade me in public, and it was one of those nice gestures of him that I truly admired.

Back in the privacy of his home, he made me feel twice as special just like when we were in public a few hours earlier. He pampered me and treated me like a VIP guest; inviting me to join him in his backyard pool, offering me iced tea and lemonade afterwards, and satisfying my sexual cravings and urges once inside his bedroom. "Mike giveth what Vanessa wantedth," was how I fondly phrased his actions, in Shakespearean fashion.

Like Carl, Mike was generous enough to offer his big, beefy behind as a teaser, to further elevate my libido, eventually turning the night into a marathon of sexual pleasures and gratification. Unlike Carl though, Mike would satisfy me twice. Maybe he knew that because I was so addicted to his *prized possession*, one orgasm would not be enough.

After our most delightful activity of the evening, we would clean up, go back to bed, have a last sip of our bottled iced tea, cuddle up, watch Nick at Nite reruns of MASH or Three's Company, and doze off. In the early hours of the morning, while my host was still in deep slumber, I would quietly leave, driving home with an irreplaceable smile on my face, welcoming what was to become a beautiful day—for me, at least.

Italian Dream Came True

Italy is a country famous for its beautiful arias and gorgeous scenery. It's also a country known to produce not just the world's best wines, but also some of the world's finest men. From Rudolph Valentino to Fabio, there is no shortage of attractive Italian men.

Michael Cantalioni was by far the handsomest and sexiest Italian-American man I dated. We met in the summer of 2000, during the exciting days of the Sydney Olympics. He was also a respondent to my Yahoo! Personals profile. He was twenty-six years old at the time and looking mighty fine.

Vinz, as he preferred to be called, invited me at his Elan Apartments unit along Montague Expressway in San Jose. He had a girlfriend at the time, and fortunately for both of us, the latter was out shopping. Vinz was totally free to play even for a couple of hours.

When I arrived at his apartment around two in the afternoon, Vinz was wearing nothing except his gym shorts. It was apparent that he had been working out because his body was still sweaty, and his Bowflex equipment was out in the living room. Seeing his manly sweat run down his athletic body only made the "green blood" in my veins boil intensely. After the traditional exchange of pleasantries when meeting someone for the first time, Vinz and I exchanged some sexual skills.

Years later, in one of his scarce e-mail messages, Vinz would recall our first meeting with gusto, accompanied by the most flattering comment regarding one's sexual performance: that mine was the "best blow job" he had ever received.

I shall also include that Vinz visited me at a relative's house in Milpitas in the winter of 2001. I was house-sitting at the time. It was a major risk I took because that relative of mine was not the most accepting when it came to my being gay. Regardless, I seized the opportunity and had a very kinky time with my Pontiac Sunfire-riding guest. Sometimes the risk-taking is worthwhile and the experience turns out to be very memorable.

Vinz and I also met in the next two years. Twice he rented a room at the Travelodge Inn by Calaveras Boulevard in 2002 and 2003, respectively. During those meetings, I experienced nothing but a sky-high level of sexual excitement and pleasure, enhanced by Vinz's beautiful face and smooth alabaster skin—major turn ons for me. I couldn't ask for more. My Italian dream came true. I had my own Fabio to smile about.

I never heard again from Vinz after our January 2003 tryst. In early 2007, some internet searches I made gave me unconfirmed results that Vinz is now an attorney working for a reputable firm in Orange County. If that's the case, I'm very proud of him. He deserves the best in life, just like how he made me feel during those times when we'd see each other; that I completely deserved all the pleasuring he gave me.

The Baldwin Years

Ever told yourself once when you were so madly, crazy in love with someone "This is the one"? I did, and for the first time in my life my instincts failed me. I realized one could never ever decipher the true mind of that special someone in your life. Even couples who have been married for several decades lose grip on their marriage vows and file for divorce.

From September 2001 to March 2005, my world revolved around Mark Baldwin. I thought he was the one; the antidote to the despair and disappointment I felt caused by the previous men I met. It took me a good four years before I realized ours was not 'the one' relationship I was so proud of.

Like the "Young Guns" in my life, I met Mark through Yahoo! Personals. He responded to my Profile and we agreed to meet on September 7, 2001.

We met at the Days Inn in Santa Clara, California along El Camino Real and Lafayette. The minute I walked in the room and saw him half naked (with only his dark blue Adidas track pants on), I became instantly aroused and fell head over heels for him. It was a combined feeling of "I want to *have* him now" and "I want a relationship with this guy."

Physically, he passed with flying colors. His alabaster skin, in contrast to his dark brown hair and hazel eyes, were perfect qualities I found in a very good-looking man. He had a striking resemblance to *Mad Men* star Jon Hamm. He had a tall, slim figure with less body hair. Smooth, shaved body parts of men are a huge turn on for me. I have to admit, he was one of the sexiest men I met that year.

So, in September 2001, Mark and I met for the first time and had an awesome night together. After that one encounter, I was quick to dismiss it as another one-night stand. Deep inside me though, it was love at first sight. I was absolutely smitten by Mark.

To my surprise, I received a call from him two days after the horrific 9/11 tragedies. I could still clearly remember his lines, word per word: "Hi Vanessa. How are you? This is Mark. What do you think of what happened last Tuesday? Lots of crazy things happening in the world now huh?"

I wasn't able to respond right away. I was overjoyed. I was in ecstasies. I also treated that phone call as a precursor to a second date. I felt like floating on air, forgetting other things, just like how Cinderella acted the next day after an enchanting evening with the Prince.

He then asked if he could see me again. I agreed without a tinge of hesitation. The following Saturday we met again, and from then on, our dates became frequent.

As the months went on, I started to know Mark a lot better. I admit that knowing him personally at this latter stage would be considered long overdue (when two individuals have been seeing each other for quite sometime already). I suppose it's a natural occurrence when someone is so smitten by a very good-looking individual with oozing sex appeal. One pays less attention to the basics about him (family, career, hobbies, etc.); at least that was the case with me. We never really engaged in lengthy conversations. Sexual delight was the main agenda in most of our meetings. We were enjoying each other's bodies so much, busying our mouths on other preoccupations.

In due time, I got to know Mark a little better. He also shared his thoughts and views on other things. It was a dramatic change from how he presented himself months before: reserved, quiet and very discreet.

He cradled his privacy in the most protective way. At the time, I knew he had a girlfriend, but didn't talk much about her. He also had a family to worry about, not to mention his friends. He worked as a technician/specialist for this biotech company in South San Francisco. He had a brother whom he shared a house with in Belmont, California, near Ralston Avenue.

He never clarified the status of his parents' marriage (he never spoke of his mother), but I've been informed that his father lived in Sacramento. Mark enjoyed riding his motorcycles and racing them. He liked going to Lake Tahoe to ski and do other recreational activities. When we first met, he had a black Ford F150 pick up truck, and sometime in 2003, he traded it for a silver Expedition.

I consider 2002 up till the early part of 2005 an exciting period of my relationship with Mark. Those are the halcyon days I continue to look back on and cherish up to this day. They remain unparalleled. We were both passionate lovers and we always made sure we pleased and satisfied each other very well. I had no complaints at all.

Mark was a very giving and enthusiastic lover. He made sure my happiness and satisfaction came first. Although our dates were only limited to the hotel room, his Belmont bedroom or his friends' houses in San Mateo (on Claremont Street and Denali Court), I must admit those were the most memorable and happy times I had with him.

In the darkness of the night and solemnity of those rooms, we became one. We were making love like horny teenagers.

There were also times when we made love in our SUVs: his spacious Ford Expedition or my Toyota Land Cruiser. The main reason for this was, we were being practical. We both knew we wouldn't have a lengthy amount of time together, so why pay for a hotel room. We realized that after a short period of time, we would have to part ways after all because he would need to go home and get some sleep. Also, hotel rooms could get pricey, and despite the fact that Mark was making good money from his job, I didn't want to take advantage of it. There were also some occasions when I did pay for our hotel room. This would happen if Mark didn't have enough time to leave work during his break time to book a room in person.

Those "car dates" turned out to be some of the most memorable and kinky times we had. Imagine the slightly bent and arched positions we put our bodies in. Such a trying experience. Regardless, they proved to be very erotic. The memories are guaranteed to make my winter nights warm.

Being with someone you really like is a breath of fresh air. The anticipation is like the much-awaited downpour on a field experiencing a dry spell. It is very stimulating. Every single moment is in bloom like a fresh flower. How I wish those moments never ended.

Mark accepted and appreciated me for who I am, and treated me like the beautiful, "sexy tranny" he had come to know me. He was one of the nicest men I met.

Mark and I had great, hot sex all the time. We did it all: bedroom sex, car sex, sex in the shower, sex at the office, light bondage and many different, kinky positions. By knowing him, I, in turn, was able to unleash the kinky fantasies I had. They all came into play whenever Mark and I played. With Mark, I was able to make those fantasies happen, and he helped me make them even more exciting along the way, enhancing the scenes in full steam.

The only scene we never tried was a *menage-a-trois*, which didn't bother me much because, in the first place, I was not into women, and secondly, Mark himself was a handful already. There was *no* need for another bedroom companion.

Mark relished the different kinds of pleasuring I gave his body. His baby-smooth hiney thoroughly enjoyed it. He was so sensitive in that area.

On our first night of intimacy—September 7, 2001—he was able to orgasm for four times. Mark undoubtedly enjoyed the oral pleasures he received from me. After a marathon of pleasuring that lasted for five hours, the redness in his eyes was enough to convey the message: he achieved sexual bliss that night.

If I made Mark very happy on that warm September night, instinctively, he made me very happy too. I was quick to conclude that we had a connection; a sort of chemistry that was undeniable. It was the kind of result that I hoped for. It was anathema to all those one-night stands I had. From then on, I started to feel more than just sexual attraction for him.

With Mark, I thought I found a new kind of hope for my lonely heart. Even though he never expressed feelings of love and togetherness, I was happy and content with the fact that I had him as a lover and friend. We never had big arguments or those so-called 'lovers' quarrel'; although sometime in March 2004 we did not speak to each other for a good two weeks because of a minor misunderstanding. When two individuals' strength of personality and pride collide, the result could be disastrous.

Sometime in early March, Mark phoned me, and when I said "Hello," his instant reply was "Natalia!" It had been a natural reaction of mine to feel insulted and affronted when the guy I am with mentions another woman's name, and Mark was no exception. I was offended, but didn't show my true feelings right away. Instead, I decided to give Mark the silent treatment.

In the ensuing days, whenever he would send instant messages while I was online, I ignored him. There was even one occasion when I chose not to entertain his recurring instant messages for hours straight no matter how many times he tried to get my attention. It was an outer display of rebellion, but deep inside I was torn apart. "How could I do this to the guy I'm madly in love with?" I asked myself.

I did, however, compose an e-mail stating my disappointment over the afore-mentioned phone conversation. I also included snippets of some slight senti-ments I had in the past which I previously let pass. This included one occasion when he ignored my offer for a dinner date, and him not showing up on my birthday dinner in May 2002.

Later that month, my friend, Lucy, and I went to Los Angeles for a short vaca-tion. Saddened, bothered and still bewildered by what happened, I thought the trip would be some sort of therapy. True enough, it was a remedy that made me forget things.

In LA, I had the most relaxing and rejuvenating time. For the first time, Mark was out of my mind. Lucy and I visited Rodeo Drive in Beverly Hills, cruised along famous thoroughfares like Santa Monica and Sunset boulevards, and hung out at a fancy bar inside the Wilshire Grand Hotel. I had a blast.

On the last night of our stay in LA, while on my way back to the hotel, I had a phone call from Mark. It was a big surprise. His first three words were "Vanessa, I'm sorry."

I was teary eyed, but they were tears of joy. Just by hearing his voice made me emotional. I remember trying my very best to speak to him with absolute compo-sure. Deep inside me, I was celebrating; my heartbeat going fast like Jeff Gordon at Daytona, my smile way up to my ears. I ultimately accepted his apology and accepted him back into my life.

The months that followed had been fairly harmonious. We resumed our regu-lar phone conversations, exchange of e-mails, and, of course, our dates. Phone and online communication were nonstop. Three times a month we would meet, and as always, have great sex. Those were very special times. Mark and I were like a boyfriend-girlfriend tandem, without the commitment. For a while it worked, until March 2005 came. It was the last time I saw him and heard from him.

There is no tinge of denial when I sum it up as an abrupt end to a flourishing relationship. I had no choice but to accept Mark's decision: to focus on his het-erosexual relationship and make it work. Had he given me an option, I would have liked for him to retain our friendship and remain in my life, regardless of the amends and adjustments I had to make.

Apparently, he married his girlfriend in December 2004 and wanted to settle for good. For a person with very good instincts, it would not take long for me to figure out that the end of a relationship was nearing. I had seen it coming and over time I learned to accept the fact.

I suppose those past, sad experiences from the previous lovers I had gave me nerves of steel, especially when it came to dealing with the pain of abandonment. In that brief chapter of my life involving Mark, I realized I was not so devastated after all. I proved resilient in some way. Only the human nature of post-break up sadness and longing plagued me, but it did not last long.

I still possess the e-mail printout of Mark's step by step instructions on how to get to his office. It is a portentous piece of paper that I vow to keep for a very long time. The workplace encounter was the last time I saw, kissed, pleased and embraced him. Should I eventually decide to include it on my scrapbook, it would serve as a reminder of how I gave unconditional love to someone and never complained for not getting any in return.

Slowly but surely, my wounded heart healed. I think when one possesses forgiveness in their heart and chooses to exercise it, the broken heart mends on its own, and in the end, you realize your life simply has to go on.

In 2005, I was already twenty-eight years old; far more mentally and emotionally mature than other people my age, I suppose. I knew how to handle painful things in life and deal with cruel blows, and am proud to say I did so with courage and dignity. Thanks to the inspiration I drew from Daddy. Where others would have lived like a recluse and indulged in destructive habits like drugs and alcohol, even commit suicide—to end the suffering—the manner which I dealt with my defeat was completely the opposite.

Always confident and possessing an ever transcendent positive attitude, I channeled my energy on working, spending more time with good friends and devotion to family, particularly with my baby nephew, Dylan, whose July 29 birthday constantly reminds me that just like the phoenix, I have to rise and take my place in the sun. July 29 is also Mark's birthday.

August 2002, New York; with my sisters

February 2003, Manila; with Mommy and 2 clowns

February 2003, Manila; after Regine Velasquez's concert, with my Aunt
Martie

February 2003, Cavite resort (Philippines); with Mommy and relatives

March 2003, dining out in Makati City (Philippines); with Mommy and relatives

June 2003, Coronado Island; with my sisters

March 2004, in Reno

July 2004, in Redding CA; with my sisters

July 2004, in Redding CA; lunching with Mommy

September 2004, Cache Creek casino; with my friend Maude

December 2004, Fremont CA; dinner with Grandma

April 2005, Disneyland, LA: with Minnie Mouse

June 2005, Washington D.C.; at the Lincoln Memorial

June 2005, Philadelphia; standing by the Liberty Bell

June 2005, Washington D.C.; at the Ella Fitzgerald exhibit

October 2005, Fremont CA; with my friend Larissa (left) and others

Christmas Day 2005 with my siblings and nephew Dylan

New Year's Eve 2005 with Maude

January 2006, Cupertino CA; with my friend Lucy

September 2006, Union City CA; with my friend Irma

November 2006, San Diego CA; with Mommy and my sisters

May 2007, Fremont CA; my 30th birthday party

May 2007; my birthday party group shot

1980, Manila; a carnival ride with my brother and Daddy.

July 2007, Milpitas CA; with friends Larissa and Abigail
(first two from the left)

8

Be My Guest

"In-calls" or the act of a massage client coming to the home or clinic of his or her therapist proved to be lucrative for my career as a Massage Therapist. However, the money I earn go to basic expenses such as food, clothing and bills; the rest I send to my poor and needy relatives in the Philippines. My in-calls took place at a rented hotel room.

I began my in-calls in December 2004. I find it more convenient and profitable because it saves my car gas (from all that driving to different, distant cities) and saves me time. Instead of wasting 30 minutes (or even one hour) on driving, I could be just spending it on massaging a client. Having a space I could rent to practice my work was the most practical option.

Some Tuesdays I would rent out a room at this discreet and quiet hotel in Fremont. Aside from conducting massage work, I would also "hold court" there (a term I fondly use which means having myself pleased and entertained by visiting lovers). By twelve o'clock in the afternoon, I am ready to accommodate my subjects, be it a client or a lover.

Like the future, there is no assurance of things that lay ahead. You don't know if it's going to be good or bad. I just keep my fingers crossed and always hope for the best. Fortunately, fate had been favorable to me. The men (friends and clients alike) who would come by were all nice and normal. I didn't encounter any "crazies." In between my massage appointments, I would summon a handsome man to keep me company and relaxed.

These men obviously fell in the bisexual category—involved with women in their long-term relationships, but at the same time interested in and inclined to having sexual romps with another male or a transsexual. They had no qualms about seeing me, and I, in turn, was most welcoming to the idea. With bisexual men, it was a free-to-be-you-and-me experience; no issues, no drama, just pure fun and pleasure.

One of the early birds (with a very nice *beak*) who would visit my nest and entice me into doing all kinds of erotic and kinky things was a guy from Milpitas named Marc. Thirty-three years old and works for a high tech company, he was not a massage client, rather an "appetizer." It's a term I use in describing men who are only good for quickie sex. Marc had a regular girlfriend at the time, but she apparently did not want to engage in the kinky sexual activities that Marc was so addicted to. Like Carl and Mike, Marc loved his *derriere* caressed, spanked and tickled, and his girlfriend simply did not want anything to do with it. It was an esoteric fetish Marc found in me. He knew I was the most qualified to perform it. Although lacking in height and athletic physique, he had a nicely shaped, meaty behind. He also had a cute *baby* face.

Another favorite guest of mine was Neil, a handsome young man in his mid-twenties who was of Armenian descent. He was one of my "originals"—the bevy of young men I had the privilege of meeting and *having* since their late teenage years. Barely nineteen when I first met him in April 2000, Neil have not changed a bit in terms of attitude and performance. I always end up floating on air every time he casts his magical spells and skills on my body. His skills had ameliorated over the years, and it had been a most exciting and erotic experience. Best of all, he had always been the nice, respectful young man he was since the first day I met him. He possessed exotic beauty, just like the faraway land where he came from. I never get tired of him.

Whenever I'm in that tiny sanctuary of mine in Fremont, I have an uninterrupted peace of mind. I am able to relax freely. Ironically, I'm also free to make any kind of noise or movement. I would sing my lungs out or dance naked in front of the vanity mirror—personal freedoms that elude me when I'm at home; maybe because there were eight people in our house at the time and so the privacy was somewhat limited.

Periodically, my guests would come by and after the fun and pleasure, I would lead them to the door, kiss them good-bye and jump back to bed feeling renewed and rejuvenated.

If the massage service I give to my clients is their therapy, the sex I get from my unselfish guests is *my* therapy. As human beings with limited strengths and common susceptibility to stress and fatigue, we definitely need a break, and I'm glad I get mine.

I would always rent a room in the outer part of the hotel compound so I could visually enjoy the beauty and serenity of the hillside view of the 680 freeway, with its trees and flowers, and the occasional chirping of the birds.

This particular scene is made even more pleasant when my friend, Lawrence, walks in. Tall, handsome and mature, at fifty, Lawrence could be mistaken for forty. He both possessed youthful looks and a higher level of libido. Residing in Livermore, California and works for an electrical company in Fremont, Lawrence is a divorce` with two sons from a previous marriage. He currently has a live-in girlfriend fifteen years his junior, and apparently, based on Lawrence's bedroom tales, his partner performs poorly.

I pride myself with dexterity when it comes to giving pleasure. I remain unrivaled. Ninety-nine percent of the men I dated have complained about their "boring" or "clueless" partners; and ninety-nine percent of them had nothing but high praises and compliments when it came to my work in the bedroom. Sometimes I'd feel sorry for those wives and girlfriends because of the unwarranted comments my male guests make about them. Sometimes I just turn my head in embarrassment and politely ask them to drop the conversation.

Lawrence was a big fan of my very stimulating oral skills. He was also a very giving lover. Like Marc, he made sure I was pleased and satisfied first. He would come by around four in the afternoon, give me my "afternoon delights," and take off a little after five.

In the early evening, my younger and more handsome guests would come by. Ronnie Harper would be the first in my own "Evening Edition" of guests. Though I didn't know much about him except for the fact that he was the prettiest boy in Fremont, and that he liked riding motorcycles, intimately, I have discovered his body's erogenous zones, using my expertise in man-pleasing. Proof of this is quite visible whenever I see him lick his lips and hear him moan in the most lustful manner. Ronnie was always on cloud nine every time he visited. Tall, with an athletic build, baby-faced with alabaster skin, Ronnie was definitely easy on the eyes. He was the quiet type of guy; did not have too much to say, but very generous in giving me pleasure. Sometimes he could be just passive—laying down in the most comfortable position, with arms and elbows behind his head; his 6 foot long body laid out like a buffet table in front of me, hot and ready for consumption.

Another handsome white boy to distract my evening solitude in Fremont was Chris Flanerty: arguably the most beautiful thing that came out of the city of San Jose. With his Abercrombie & Fitch model-like looks, a Hollywood heartthrob face, and NBA player-like height, this thirty year-old hunk of a man no doubt commands attention from both women and men. I just feel luckier than all those men and women because I get to enjoy and appreciate Chris first-hand. There was no need for me to fantasize.

One slight skirmish with my meetings with Chris was the recurring issue of STD and other diseases. He was so paranoid over those things. Although we have consistently practiced safe sex, at the end of our *session*, he would repeatedly ask me if I had been tested.

I always declare, not only to Chris but to the other lovers as well, that I am totally clean and disease-free. Every six months, I would visit a clinic in San Jose to get tested. Thankfully, results always come out negative.

I know myself better than anyone. I always make it a point to Chris that he should never doubt my statements. In the end, my assertiveness seems to calm and quiet him.

Sometimes he confuses me whenever he brings up the matter because on some occasions, he would perform sexual acts with me that are unsafe and risky. Regardless, the nights I shared with Chris were some of the most sexually gratifying I had.

Occasionally, he would even invite me to his apartment near Downtown San Jose to play. This would only happen when his ever-snooping girlfriend is out of town or sleeping in her own apartment. Despite those minor restrictions, I'm just glad that when it comes to access on Chris' body, there are no restrictions for me.

Not only Chris was blessed with dashing good looks, he also possessed good attitude and temperament. He had a sweet, charismatic tongue. There's always enthusiasm in his tone. He would start our conversation with "Hey beautiful" or "Hey sexy"; utter complimentary phrases in the bedroom such as "You're amazing" or "You're the best." They were all flattering. One could tell that the boy knows how to show respect to others, and knows how to appreciate a very talented girl like me.

I feel so lucky for having lovers who are just plain nice, unselfish and open minded. They have the right moves and words. They know how to touch and tease me, and above all, they guarantee my happiness and satisfaction.

At that point, I already knew how to play the game. I was not so naïve and passive as before. In the early years of my *womanhood* I was the duck being hunted, but these days the table has turned. Gone are the days when I would date average-looking men with below average character; men who are selfish—always taking pleasure and not giving me any; and hypocritical men—those who are embarrassed to be seen in public with me and judging me for not being "very passable," but at the same time benefiting from my bedroom talents.

This time around, my choice and decisions are given much importance. I could choose to delight myself with someone I fancy, or decline another's company. I realize now that I don't belong in the shadow of any man anymore, nor I have to be content to stay inside his car, crumpling myself down because of the fear of being seen with a transsexual.

I learned that I could turn things around and have men chasing me instead of me chasing them. Just like an appetizer, I have something special and addicting, something tempting and enticing, which makes men beg for more. I realize now that I could be the 'main entrée', the main event, the center of it all.

9

The Other Men

International Delights

"I have *tasted* all the delicacies of Western and Eastern Europe" I like to brag sometimes. It was like initiating my own Congress of Vienna, only this time the participants were younger, more handsome, admirable in physique and without a doubt, promiscuous.

Just like my passion and interest in the study of European history, my passion and lust for its men is just as flaming. I always fall prey to those Teutonic specimen. Surprisingly, I seem to enjoy the way they take control of me and my senses.

It has been a universally known fact that Europeans are the most open-minded, liberal group of people in existence, and I appreciate that. With these German, Austrian and Scandinavian men, I never had to deal with the struggle for acceptance.

Homosexual, bisexual, and transgender figures have graced their society since time immemorial: Alexander the Great, Richard III, Queen Christina of Sweden and the Abbe Francois Timoleon de Choisy to name a few. Therefore, I knew for a fact that their encounter with me was just another normal occurrence. These men were so tolerant and open-minded they easily opened their hotel and apartment doors for me as well.

The first of these "Blue-eyed booties" (a term I fondly called their group) whose company I thoroughly enjoyed was thirty year-old Markus Zeber of Palo Alto, California. He was the epitome of a true European: well-mannered, drank wine like water, smoked like a chimney, and, of course, tall, blond and blue-eyed. He was very good-looking and very kinky as well.

From 2003 to the early part of 2004, we regularly met. I would come over to his house near University Avenue, and after a brief *tete-a-tete* upon my arrival, he would inebriate me with several glasses of wine and start his teasing and seducing tactics.

He liked wearing thong underwear and enjoyed taking pictures of his sexual activities. He most definitely enjoyed the company of Asian women and transsexuals. At one point, he even suggested a *ménage-a-trois* with another girl. It never happened. Since 2005, I have not heard from him.

Our final meeting back in the fall of 2004 was a bit amusing. Knowing that his girlfriend was in San Francisco, watching the Broadway musical *Mama Mia*, Markus asked me to come over to fill in that space when he'd be by himself. He was not the type of guy to be left alone with his own *devices*. We not only filled our glasses with wine, but also filled the hour with some of the best and kinkiest sex I ever had.

Another *Deutschlander* I dated was forty year-old Heinz Oberer. Unlike Markus, this particular Mr.Blue Eyes was a permanent resident of Germany who visited the Bay Area for business periodically. Sometime in early 2005, he invited me to his nice suite at the De Anza Hotel in Downtown San Jose.

I came by, we had wine and a very pleasurable time. Just like Markus, he had a penchant for dirty, kinky sexual activities. His fantasies were more disgusting. He wanted to try *golden* (and *brown*) *showers*. Several months after we met, he sent me another e-mail telling me he would be in town again, and that this time he would like us to do those nasty things in the bedroom. It never materialized, for that was the last time I heard from him.

My sexual relations and experiences with European men were not limited to Germans alone. From Russian men, there was love for sex with Vanessa as well. The most loyal of them all was Alexander. Though born in Russia, he spoke English with the slightest Russian accent. He was definitely a lot younger than his German counterparts.

Alexander would keep me company in my hotel room in Fremont from time to time. Although there were times his visits became an interruption to my in-call massage work, I had no complaints. He pleased me and it made me happy. His disarming topaz eyes were enough to keep me coming back for more of his warm, sexy touch.

Beautiful men and their bodies are some of my greatest weaknesses, and in the back of my mind, a handsome thing making time for me and keeping me company even for a short period of time brings a certain kind of validation—that I am *worthy* of his time. It meant a lot to me.

Gal Dober from Bosnia was another favorite visitor. An art dealer from Emeryville, he had a special affiliation with Filipinos because he said his number one customers were from the Filipino-American community. "They're crazy about artworks and paintings from Europe," he claimed. No wonder he had a special affection towards me, despite the fact that there were obviously other transsexuals out there of different nationalities who were prettier than me.

Gal was over six feet tall, with an Atlas-like frame, very typical of those Eastern European bodybuilders who model for numerous muscle websites on the internet. I simply loved his body. Being a tall-framed girl myself, I prefer men who are the same height as mine or taller.

Through art, Gal and I found a common connection: he enjoyed my artistry in pleasing a man, and I fancied his gorgeous body as a work of art.

I tip my hat to the person who coined the phrase "Turkish delight" because it certainly is a very delightful and *delicious* thing to have.

My one and only Turkish delight was not found in Ankara or Istanbul, rather in the city of Fremont. Gino was his name. Never have I experienced such pleasure and pampering, Eastern style.

Although young at age (he was only twenty-five when I met him in late 2005), Gino already had a sense of maturity and hospitality. He knew how to entertain and accommodate a guest.

Aside from initially showing genuine politeness and pleasant manners, his sybaritic flair was all too apparent. He would lay out the best cigarettes (imported), and the most expensive and rare alcoholic beverages for me. They were absolutely better-tasting than some of their American counterparts.

But Gino also had far better qualities. Coming from a well-to-do family in Istanbul, Gino not only knew how to live a lavish lifestyle, he also prioritized the comfort and pleasure of his guests.

His high tastes and privileged family background were evident at his Fremont home. The furniture inside were all made with mahogany wood; his queen-size bed had an Eastern flavor to it—with canopies of silk and satin on all four ends; and the fabric and pillow covers were Bohemian in design. His sound system was state-of-the-art; his personal computer and other "hi-tech" gadgets were all brand new. Gino definitely poured in a lot of money to acquire a lavish lifestyle.

His bedroom was filled with enticing scents from a bevy of aromatic candles. It was the perfect setting for a perfect Saturday evening at home. What was more captivating was the presence of this handsome creature with big brown eyes and flawless skin, standing before me—Gino. With his lustful stare and inviting smile, Gino was simply irresistible.

With Gino, it was mutual attraction. He responded to my Casual Encounters ad on Craigslist in November 2005. For some reason, our meeting never materialized. I was very busy with my endless massage appointments at the time, and every time Gino would call or send instant messages online asking me to meet him, I declined.

One night that November, someone called me for a massage appointment, gave me directions to his house in Fremont, and when the person opened the door, to my surprise and embarrassment, it was Gino. I recognized his face instantly because of the picture he sent me via e-mail weeks earlier. I was both embarrassed and excited. It was a shame that we had to meet that way. I apologized to him, explaining that I had been very busy the past few weeks with work. Gino, being the gentleman that he was, assured me it was alright.

On the night we met, every thing he did was right. It was a prelude to two more meetings filled with fun and kinky sex. Gino, just as he was in the living room, made sure I was very happy and satisfied in his bedroom as well.

In January 2006, Gino was scheduled to fly back to Turkey, for good. The Turkish army summoned him in late 2005 back to service. A week before, on Christmas Day, we met for the last time. I gave him a Christmas card with my picture enclosed, and a wallet as a parting gift. In a return gesture, he gave me a silver candelabra.

It was not the last souvenir I had of him though. On our second date (in late November), he burned a CD for me with songs of my favorite Filipino singer, Regine Velasquez. I considered it a very special act of kindness from a person I hardly knew. It struck a chord in me because no other man I met before made the time or go through the trouble to do such thing. Others just didn't have the time, simply did not care or didn't even bother asking who my favorite artist was from my native country in the first place. It was an unprecedented act and definitely unforgettable.

Wherever Gino is today, rest assured he will always be in my heart and mind. I have his underwear to touch and feel; to remind me of his warm, smooth skin rubbing against mine during those three sizzling fall and winter nights we had. I have the shiny silver candelabra to remind me of the sparkle in his brown eyes, and I have that CD of Regine whose songs arouse feelings of want and desire through their sweet and sentimental lyrics. Gino was my one and only Turkish delight.

Men in Uniform

Once when having a conversation with my late uncle, Tony, about military life, he reminded me about Daddy's suggestion back in 1996 that I join the Navy. My response to uncle was "I'd rather date them than join them."

My dear uncle was in stitches over that remark. Of my three uncles—Manny, Mario and Tony—Uncle Tony had the most sense of humor.

The first of the dozens of men in uniform whom I dated was US Army officer and air marshal Gerald Fallon. This very good-looking soldier responded to my Yahoo! Personals profile in late 2001. He was stationed in Florida at the time, and we would regularly communicate through e-mail and occasional phone conversations.

Gerald was by the far the handsomest military guy I dated—for the '30 and up' category. He resembled John Stamos in some way. I love dark men with dark, good looks. There was no denying that Gerald's pretty face, matched by his very macho profession, turned me on a great deal.

In July 2002, Gerald was ordered to perform air marshal duties on flights from Florida to Los Angeles, in the wake of the heightened security efforts stemming from the recent 9/11 attacks. It was also the perfect time to meet him. Weeks prior, he suggested I drove to Los Angeles to meet him. He explained to me that that was the best way for us to meet, since he didn't know if he'd ever fly to San Francisco (which in turn was a lot closer to where I lived).

Seizing this great opportunity to be with a decorated Army officer, I acquiesced to Gerald's plans. In late July, I traveled to LA, ending up in Manhattan Beach where Gerald was staying at the Holiday Inn hotel.

Due to the fact that he won't arrive at the hotel until later in the evening, Gerald gave the front desk staff specific instructions to provide me with an extra key, so that if ever I arrived earlier than my host, I'd gain access to his room and would be able to rest and relax. The friendly front desk staff obliged, and true enough, I arrived hours earlier than my host. Inside Gerald's room, I was able to unwind before what was to become a very tiring night-time *activity*.

When Gerald arrived around 9 in the evening, he was tired, but still managed to pull out some energy so that we could have some fun. After some warm hugs and hellos upon entering the room, Gerald undressed, rested his gun atop the vanity table, took a shower and took me to *heaven* afterwards.

It was a one-night stand with Gerald, but the fun I had with him, along with his kind personality, would always stay in my memory. It was such an irony for me to realize that despite the macho qualities of his profession—surrounded by guns and bombs—he still possessed that certain gentle charisma not found in many men these days. I sometimes think that the reason why Gerald became a decorated Army officer was due to the fact that he knew how to treat people well; that he knew how to communicate and relate with his fellow soldiers.

The last time I heard from Gerald was in March 2003, while he was stationed in Iraq. He would send me e-mails along with some pictures of adult nature which I found very entertaining. One of those pictures was him naked cropped over the front cover of *Playgirl* magazine; obviously computer-enhanced.

Wherever he is now, I really hope he didn't become another casualty of that ridiculous, unwanted war.

Nick Ramirez was an Alameda County sheriff. Though not thoroughly handsome like Gerald, Nick possessed the priceless quality of companionship.

From summer to fall of 2002, Nick and I dated. We shared many wonderful dates, from lunches to dinners, and going to the movies. One memorable date I had with Nick was when we saw the *James Bond 007* movie Die Another Day at the Shoreline Theaters in Mountain View, California. Before the movies, we ate at the El Burro Mexican restaurant in Newark, about half an hour away.

Nick also worked as a part time realtor. He owned and managed a realty company which specialized on foreclosures. He even brought me to his office one time in Pleasanton, California, and became furious when he found out that one of his staff members forgot to bring some important documents which were crucial to their company meeting in LA the following week.

Nick was like me in temperament. We're both Taureans. We enjoyed good food and good company. We both enjoyed sex as well. We also loathed stupid, inefficient people, especially some drivers on the road who were completely clueless behind the wheel.

Being a passenger of him in his Ford Taurus for many times, I witnessed Nick's frustrations when it came to bad drivers sharing the road with him. He would execute a litany of curses at them.

By early 2003, I rarely saw Nick because I was in a serious relationship with my then-boyfriend, Ron Hubert. By 2004, our relationship was non-existent. He became very busy with his two jobs and I became busy with my studies and other dates.

It was fair game. Nick needed time to focus on his new business venture, and I needed time to explore other possible relationships and adventures.

Alex Holstein was a thirty-five year-old San Jose police officer I briefly dated in 2004.

He was about 5'10" tall and of mixed race: half-white, half-Mexican. He had a nice build and an even nicer butt. This handsome cop was married, so naturally, he didn't have a lot of time and freedom to be with me.

Our first meeting took place at the drive-in theaters along Capitol Expressway in San Jose. We had a nice time. I really enjoyed what I *saw*.

We would also rendezvous at the San Jose Main Jail parking lot during his break time and have some "car fun," and twice he had me over at his Campbell, California home while the wife was at work. Those were fun times.

But just like the nature of his chosen profession, Alex was constantly at risk and taking risks. But his risk-taking is what I admire about him the most. He was brave enough to do things with me even if he knew the possibility of being caught was imminent.

Trent Adkins

For the great Franklin Delano Roosevelt, December 1941 would "live in infamy." Sixty years later, it was all a different story—for me. In December 2001, I had the most unforgettable experience in all my dating years. It was an experience unparalleled in the broadest dimensions. My heart always beats faster and I smile like there is no tomorrow whenever I reminisce the events that took place on that one special night.

It happened in the eclectic city of Los Angeles, in the company of a handsome young man from the US Navy, Trent Adkins. Although it has been five years since that experience, the memories of an undoubtedly enchanting evening still reign in my nostalgic mind. If I should be given permission to have my own Hall of Fame, Trent would be the Chairman of the Board.

Tall, slim and blond, with light blue eyes that were both piercing and disarming, Trent was the epitome of an all-American boy. In the world stage, the 'American boy' is the cynosure; he is the eye candy of hot-blooded teenage girls, and his clothing style is emulated by his male counterparts living on all four corners of the globe. To me, Trent was not just the all-American boy, he was the coolest American boy I ever met. He was my very own Justin Timberlake—young, handsome and oozing with sex appeal.

Knowledgeable in many forms of discussion, whether sports or science, and exceptional in bed, I couldn't ask for more. Brent possessed beauty, brains and bedroom skills. To me, nothing is more attractive and appealing than a man who could hold a conversation, regardless if he really knew what he was talking about or not. The most important thing is, I don't get bored. Trent was in a chatty mood the whole time we were driving along the 5 and 101 freeways *en route* to the LA clubs.

I remember going through a typical LA traffic jam that Saturday evening while on our way to the clubs of Santa Monica Boulevard, and not getting bored or annoyed at all just because I remained amused by the stories and short anecdotes Trent volubly shared. In his endless rants and raves, I sensed humbleness and honesty. He shared what was on his mind and was opinionated on many things, especially when it came to the social and political events of the day.

Coming from a broken family in Michigan, Trent and his pot-smoking mother and delinquent brother surprisingly got along well; except for the occasional rows between him and the latter, which was normal between siblings especially in their adolescent years. Despite the relatively peaceful co-existence between mother and sons, Trent was not the type to stay home and grow old in his hometown. He wanted a different life. He wanted to move on.

Trent was a troubled teen himself. He had always gotten into fights with other boys and had experimented with drugs and alcohol in his juvenile years. At some point in his young adult life, Trent wanted to turn things around. After graduating from high school, he enlisted in the Navy.

Trent was a US Navy E3 at the time of our meeting. He was stationed in San Diego and wanted to attend college, aiming for a degree in Dental Hygiene. He had just arrived in the US from Okinawa a few weeks earlier prior to our meeting. Naturally, hitting the bar scene and having a good time were foremost in Trent's agenda.

While still in Okinawa the previous months, Trent and I had been communicating through e-mail and online chat. From time to time, he had expressed his genuine interest to meet me upon his return to the US. He was even bold enough to tell me about his desire for us to live together in San Diego. Exciting as it may have sounded—the idea that I would be offered a position of a live-in girlfriend by a young straight guy—it just seemed impossible. Maybe it was just a spur-of-the-moment statement from Trent, heightened by his excitement over his upcoming return trip to the US, or he was just pulling my leg. Regardless, I never took the idea seriously.

The very idea that it would be Trent's first time in California, not having the slightest knowledge about the cost of living here, state laws, regulations, etc., and the sole fact that he had no prior experience when it came to living together with a girlfriend, made me realize it would be one difficult, tumultuous life for both of us. His proposal fell on deaf ears, and ultimately the subject was mooted.

All those issues aside, I started my six-hour journey to Los Angeles (by car) on the morning of December 16, 2001. It was a trip that would go down in my personal history as the most exciting and most memorable.

I arrived at the Days Inn hotel in Whittier, California around three in the afternoon. Trent was in room 108. When he opened the door, he greeted me with a "Hi" and, in turn, I introduced myself accompanied by a handshake. After the exchange of pleasantries and a brief chat, we became intimate.

There was no denying that the main objective of that meeting was fantasy fulfillment: Trent's desire to be with a transsexual for the first time, and my burning desire to be with a very good-looking young blond. It was a match made in heaven.

Trent definitely knew how to handle his ship. My body was in full steam, and I was not ready to *dock* anytime soon.

The "minutes after" were very sexy. Admiring his body with my lustful gaze, I couldn't help but comment on the interesting tattoos he had: a sun on his back, a scorpion on his left pelvic area and a circle on one his fingers. He explained to me the relevance of each of those tattoos. While he was doing that, my lips were continuously probing his biceps and shoulders and anything in between. Never have I felt so much freedom in unleashing my kinkiness. Trent let me do what I wanted, and it was definitely a new experience for me. No limits, no restrictions, no "nos."

Trent was your typical sailor—fond of tattoos, drank beer like water and possessed a spend-it-all kind of attitude. It's funny when I recall how the latter was not applicable to him that night. Trent told me he only had $200 left in his savings account and that he was planning to save it for the remaining days before payday. With him already volunteering to pay for the hotel room for two nights (even though I was only with him for one), I thought it was just fair that I covered any incurring expenses we might have on our night out.

While on our way to the clubs in LA, I got to know Trent's tastes a little bit. He liked the music of Creedence Clearwater and Dave Matthews Band. He also proudly shared some of the Japanese words and phrases he learned while in Okinawa.

Upon arriving in LA, Trent and I grabbed a bite to eat at the El Pollo Loco restaurant along Santa Monica Boulevard. I liked the way they cooked and prepared their chicken. Trent enjoyed his meal, too, and afterwards showed his gentleman-like side when he offered to clear out our table and put the tray on top of the trash can by the door.

They say the "stars shine in LA." I could very well attest to that because on the night Trent and I went bar-hopping along action-filled Santa Monica Boulevard, it seemed like the night sky paved the way for its glittering stars to shine on us. What was more enchanting was the incandescence that dominated our surroundings. For one night only, it seemed to me that almost every establishment on that particular stretch of the boulevard deliberately left their lights on in full glow as if they were the endless flashing of cameras from the paparazzi. It did not take long for me to realize that we're no different from the gallivanting Hollywood celebrities on a Saturday night. The feeling of tremendous excitement was simply inevitable. I was so proud to be in the company of Trent. He was, by far, the handsomest young man that evening. I never dared look on another guy's eyes.

Trent looked like every inch of a Hollywood celebrity that night; in fact, I thought he looked better than some young actors in La la Land. I couldn't ask for more. He was like a prized possession that I clung to—the 'trophy boy', the guy you're proud to be seen with. There was an abundance of admiring stares and lustful gaze that night as we strolled along lively Santa Monica Boulevard. Trent's ravishing good looks were the center of attention.

We went to three different establishments that were favorite hang-out places of gay men: Mickey's, 7969 and a pool bar in between. The latter would serve as the most memorable because in there, Trent kissed me several times. He also taught me how to play pool.

Every time he won a set, he came up to me and gave me a kiss. The feeling was utterly disarming, with a tingling sensation. I felt like a teeny bopper fan of a famous pop star being given VIP treatment by the pop star himself.

I had to admit, I was one step closer to falling in love. I was also aroused by it. For the second time, I wanted to make love to him.

A little after midnight, we decided to go back to the hotel and get a good night's rest. Trent asserted the need for him to wake up early because he had to report to the San Diego Naval Base by eight in the morning; a fact that disappointed me in a way. I was hoping we could stay up a little bit more and have more fun.

By one in the morning we were in bed, fooling around a little bit, and by half past two he told me "Okay, bedtime." He then set the alarm for six and then the lights were out. For some reason, I sensed an eerie message that coincided with his turning the lamp off: as the lights went out, so was the flame of hope that we would see each other again after that night.

In the early hours of that Sunday morning, we got up, showered, got dressed and said our farewells. Trent gave me a hug accompanied by a plain and simple "Good-bye." It was the last time I saw him.

It's been six years since that encounter, but the memories of the fun and pleasure we had remain as fresh as the flowers of spring. In my heart and mind, Trent will always have a special place. There is a little corner where I draw that certain joy he had given me. True, it was only for one night that we were together, but I know for a fact that I will cherish and celebrate the memories I have of him for many days and nights to come. Trent made me feel like his very special girlfriend with the genuine affection and respect he had shown.

I admire Trent for the will and courage to be seen in public with a transsexual. In a world where beauty is the main criteria for model relationships, he was proud and happy to be with an average-looking person like myself. Not to mention the fact that I was not even a genetic female. One could imagine the question marks on the minds of the conservative and close-minded people who saw us that night and easily detected my true gender despite the short, black mini skirt and high heels that I wore (which, to my delight, garnered several wolf whistles and catcalls).

Trent did not care about the prejudice and criticism that might have existed that night, rather he just cared about my happiness and pleasure. To me, such act deserves the highest form of admiration and appreciation. Trent was a young man who was actually smart enough not to fall victim to society's pressure to practice those so-called "moral standards," one of which dictates the classic and ridiculous man-and-woman-only type of intimacy.

In the years that followed, I realized the experience I had with Trent proved unparalleled. No other experience has come close to duplicating that wonderful time. Although I think about him from time to time, I am wholly content with the fact that he will always be included in my list of happy memories and extremely fun escapades. It's like opening a Faberge egg—not only it puts a big smile on your face, but it's also mesmerizing; and you can't help but dwell on its uniqueness and beauty. The feeling is the same whenever I reminisce the time I had with Trent.

Kevin Moreway

In early 2002, when I have not heard from Trent anymore, with all those voice mail messages I left him, loneliness again struck me. I vowed to move on; to move on with a new lover or *pastime*.

A "remnant" of the many replies I received from my Yahoo! Personals profile back in the summer of 2001 came from Kevin Moreway—a shy, quiet, good-looking guy from the San Jose area. I have kept his e-mail address previously and so we resumed correspondence. In one of his replies, he expressed an interest in meeting.

He suggested we met at the AMC Mercado Theaters in Santa Clara, California because he worked in that area. He told me the best time to meet him was late in the evening because that's when his shift ends.

One cold January night in 2002, I went to the theater and met Kevin. Nervous in some way because it was my first time meeting him, I didn't have the slightest idea how this encounter would unfold, although in our previous correspondence, we both agreed it would be of a sexual nature.

When Kevin came knocking on my SUV's door, I was hesitant in opening it. Eventually, I came to my senses and gave this guy the courtesy of opening the door. He hopped in and introduced himself. He was polite and soft-spoken. Underneath that gentle exterior though, lies a rough and kinky lover.

In the following months, Kevin and I would have *sexcapades* in places where he worked at. This included the restaurant in Santa Clara where he worked as a manager, and at a hotel in San Leandro, California where he was head chef.

Whenever I would pass by the Great America Parkway exit along the 101 freeway and have a glance at Tomatina's—the restaurant where Kevin used to work as a manager—the memories of the sexual romp I had there with him become lively as the bustling commercial center where it's situated.

In March 2002, a couple of months after meeting him at the Mercado theaters, Kevin and I were getting wild on top of Tomatina's kitchen counter. What better place to satiate my hunger for man-love than inside a restaurant, right? How ironic. At around eleven thirty that one evening, when all other employees have left, I walked in and voluntarily *employed* myself as Kevin's night-time *server*.

Not hearing from Trent anymore only added to the desperation. Although I was happy and content with my brief experience with him, at twenty-five, my sexual libido was at an all-time high, and I definitely yearned for more physical attention. Also, during that time, my penchant for sexual experimentation and exploration reached its zenith, so despite the "loving" I got from other regular lovers, I wanted more and wanted more "options."

The year 2002 proved to be the most memorable for me when it came to the number of sexual relations and activities I had.

Great sex at risky places with Kevin didn't end at Tomatina's. In April 2003, he was daring enough to invite me at his new workplace—the Hilton Garden Inn in San Leandro where he worked as head chef. There, he instructed me to act as if I was an applicant ready for a job interview. Unbeknownst to his co-workers, Kevin was meeting me for personal reasons rather than professional.

It turned out that hotel employees could receive concessions such as free rooms, free meals, etc., so Kevin had a nice, cozy room reserved for us.

In that particular room, we took care of our *agenda*. One must remember that by doing this, Kevin was risking his job and freedom in an enormous way. The risk of being caught in the act—and caught doing *it* at the workplace—could mean immediate removal and possibly a trip to the nearest county jail. Luckily for us, every thing went smoothly and every minute was so much fun. Like his unselfish *forebears*, he made sure I was satisfied.

For the first (and last) time, Kevin laid me in bed and made love to me. It was a most pleasurable and erotic gesture reminiscent of my *sessions* with other talented lovers. I always feel romance whenever a lover lays me down in bed. To me, it's an expression of confidence and appreciation. Not all the men I met previously had those characteristics.

Most of the time, it was all about quickies and uncomfortable sexual positions.

I leveled Kevin with his very sexy counterparts—Brian, Mark, Carl and Mike—in their exalted positions, deserving only of those few who really satisfied me from start to finish.

Yes, Kevin left quite an impression as one of the best studs qualified for my sexual needs, but not the best suited for constant companionship and a thriving man-woman relationship that have eluded me all those years.

The Hilton Garden Inn scene was the last I would see of Kevin. I never heard back from him anymore, but am happy and content with the fact that I had such wild experiences with him. There is also a feeling of accomplishment in this. The days of me giving and giving more, while not getting any satisfaction in return, are gone. By 2003, I knew I was in total control of my sexual relationships.

A Few Good Men in my Life

Not all men possess a Casanova character; certainly not in my experiences with these two who gained my utmost respect. These good men and sincere friends serve as the antidote to the feelings of prejudice and rejection I had from others. With this group, I felt care and concern for the first time. Their warmth, sincerity and compassion have enveloped my entire being and gave me a different kind of self-confidence and pride. The song *To Sir With Love* befits how I look at all of my relationships. They have unselfishly and willingly shared their wisdom and good advice, and it definitely helped me keep my feet on the ground; and on some occasions, my fists away from my adversary's face.

Jim Craven or "Daddy Jim," as I fondly and affectionately called him, was a thirty-nine year-old San Francisco native working for a hi-tech company in the East Bay. We met in the summer of 2004. He's the one man I could very well consider a big brother if ever I would be given a second chance to relive my life. From day one, I had very good instincts about him.

His sound advice on certain things proved useful and very important. Once, when I was so furious at this individual who wrote lies and malicious things about me on the internet, Daddy Jim was there to pacify me.

The culprit was a one-time date who had gone bitter on me for unknown reasons. At any rate, he continued bombarding me with atrocious remarks online to the point of libel. He wrote the most offending and damaging comments about me which were all untrue.

I mentioned the incident to Daddy Jim, and in his calm and assuring tone, he counseled "If I were you I'll just let it go." One of my mantras is "Fire cannot be put out by starting another one," so I decided to let the issue die down by itself. To make a counterattack would only mean I'm leveling myself with that disgruntled person's lowly and unworthy existence. I just couldn't afford to let that happen. I followed Daddy Jim's advice, and slowly but surely, the abusive online articles, as well as its perpetrator, disappeared from the internet world.

Good advice was not the only thing I appreciated from Daddy Jim; he was also the perfect host. I could never think of an occasion wherein I didn't have a blast. I was never bored. Our get-togethers were always some of the best times I had in recent memory.

The only regret I had was that we didn't have enough time to do it. Six to seven hours of fun and pleasure simply were not enough. I would come by on a Saturday or Sunday evening; warm hugs and beautiful roses await me. Daddy Jim would lead me to his cozy, candle-lit living room area, and after a brief *tete-at-tete* he would play the right kind of music, serve the most mouth-watering gourmet food with wine, and later engage ourselves in hours of nonstop pleasure.

When there were nights he didn't have enough time to prepare a good meal for me, we would buy dinner to-go or eat out at his favorite Thai restaurant nearby. For dessert, he would serve the best-tasting cookies. They were rich in taste and moist inside. He knew I relished such decadent desserts.

Daddy Jim constantly made me feel at home and at ease. My one hour drive to San Francisco was well worth it. He made sure I had the most enjoyable and relaxing experience.

Intuitively, I felt really cared for by him. San Francisco weather could be punishing sometimes especially during winter, and when during those freezing nights we would go out for a short walk, he made sure I was comfortably covered. He would let me wear one of his cargo pants or wool sweaters.

Daddy Jim's feline pet was as welcoming as her master. The precious companion never showed the slightest expression of dislike or discrimination towards me. I felt sad and sorry for Daddy Jim when I learned that she had to be put away in early 2006. She was his most loyal companion. Daddy Jim gave her an almost paternal-like care and protection; making sure she was fed on time, and took her to the veterinary when she was sick. Seeing his concern first-hand made me recall of the times I yearned for a father figure who would treat me good. Yearning, not anymore; celebrating the good times with Daddy Jim, yes.

Another good *daddy* I met was Michael Walton. Although ten years older than Daddy Jim, they were not so different in character and profession. Both worked for the hi-tech world and both showed genuine appreciation towards me. Like Daddy Jim, Daddy Mike was simply nice and loving.

Ours is a friendship that is still going strong from that one May day in 2004. He responded to my profile on OUTPersonals, a dating site that caters to homosexual and bisexual men, as well as the transgender. We agreed to meet for lunch at the cozy and expensive Italian restaurant in Fremont called Massimo's. After lunch, as he walked me to my car, he did something which ultimately validated the already good impression I had of him: he surprised me with a Clinique Happy perfume set. It was a belated birthday present. Although I previously mentioned to him that my birthday was days passed, I had the least notion that he would be so thoughtful and sweet to hand me a present—especially on our first date!

Daddy Mike's generosity was not limited to him giving me perfume sets. He also gave time to help me out on certain things. Whenever I had computer problems, Daddy Mike came to the rescue. He would set aside valuable time from his busy workweek, schedule a meeting at my house, and fix my computer. These simple acts of kindness definitely garnered him utmost respect from me. No other Daddy has ever done that to me, and so I just couldn't afford not to tell the world what a wonderful human being he is.

Daddy Mike is also the most religious of my other Daddies when it comes to e-mail. He keeps in touch regularly. One simple request I have of him is that he keeps me posted on the new events and developments in his life, and he has done so unfailingly.

Our communication had always been enveloped with excitement and humor. I specially enjoy hearing about his trips to Cache Creek Casino. He is a regular gambler. His stories about weird and crazy casino-goers always amuse me. The raconteur-like manner he shares such stories is even made more amusing by his funny gestures and facial expressions. He makes me laugh and that's very important. I loathe boredom.

Life is not perfect. I have heard this adage all my life and I firmly believe in it, mainly because it is so applicable to mine. Despite the fact that my own life is not perfect, after meeting these few good men, I've come to terms with reality. It's a reality which I'm very happy to live with; the fact that I have these special friends who know how to acknowledge and appreciate my being transsexual, without any tinge of reservation and inhibition. They respect me for who I am, and for what I am—passable or not—and are not ashamed to be seen with me in public. Moreover, they not only offered good company, they also shared their wisdom.

To this day, whenever I reminisce those insouciant moments with Daddy Jim while he's holding my hand as we walk side by side along Clement Street, or while Daddy Mike is caressing my hand so devotedly inside Massimo's, I feel a certain kind of warmth which not only feels so good on the exterior, but also seems to nourish and enliven my very soul.

10

According to Vanessa

Like a bird that had just been freed from her cage, I spread my wings wide, fly away gracefully and take my place in the sun. I am a new me—more confident, wiser, classier and charming than ever. I would like to share with you some fabulous routines I practice when it comes to being out there, socially.

I may not have acquired big breasts and a hormone-produced feminine face like my transsexual counterparts through thousands of dollars paid for surgery and repair, but in executing grace and showing my charming personality, I know I am right on the money. I make sure I leave a good impression to the men and women I come across with.

Image and self-representation should be held paramount. I always stood with my back straight, chin slightly up, and always had an ever-ready smile. It exudes confidence and affirms an impressionable character.

A friendly smile is quite handy and would take you places. It's also helpful when, by accident or purpose, you make eye contact with another. Through that you're sending the message that you can be approachable.

When engaged in casual conversation, I make sure I compliment the other person in some way, whether it be her blouse or his suit, and I always end the meeting with a handshake or a hug (the latter only applies to those whom I've been acquainted to before and meeting for the second time).

When asked out to lunch or dinner, one would never catch me wearing the plainest clothes. Once, when my friend, Jeff Harton, asked me out to lunch in the spring of 2005, I decided to wear a ruffled aqua-green satin blouse appropriately designed for the season—with floral prints—paired with a denim skirt and heels.

I like showing off my legs. They are long and shapely. I can not recall the many times men (and women alike) have complimented my legs. At Chili's that afternoon, I was my own witness as to how the men paused and gave me admiring stares, and the women with that 'No-she-didn't!' look. It was funny, but the men definitely flattered me. But, of course, my handsome date was first to give me compliments.

When going out to dinner and dancing, I make sure I wear my one-of-a-kind blouses. It helps in making me stand out from the crowd. I receive many compliments on the blouses I wear. Pastels and pink shades I find very appealing, as well as those with glittery fabrics.

Dinner dates have become a ritual for me and a regular occupant of my social calendar. Due to the fact that it happens during the latter part of the day, when people have become tired and haggard-looking from earlier activities (such as work, errands, etc.), I make sure my face is looking fresh and rested. I make sure the energy and glow are evident. Again, I want to stand out.

I have a simple regimen for this. Later in the afternoon, perhaps three hours before the scheduled dinner, I would de-stress myself by taking a nap while smooth jazz or instrumental music is playing on my radio; then I'd take a replenishing shower half an hour after I wake up, and start preparing myself for the evening. This gives a rested and relaxed projection on the face.

When I'm all set for my dinner date or evening soiree, it's time to welcome the fabulous experiences.

I think I have been to some of the most popular restaurants and bars in the Bay Area. Here are some of my favorites. In Fremont: the Olive Garden and Massimo's; Red Lobster and Black Angus in Milpitas; Macaroni Grill in Dublin and the Elephant Bar in Concord. When visiting San Francisco, I prefer dining out at the popular restaurants by Fisherman's Wharf. Some my favorites there are Alioto's, Tarantino's and the Boulevard by the Embarcadero.

When going out to a simple dinner, my practicality is often exercised. I would pick a restaurant that is within the neighborhood or is not too far. One does not need to waste gas, time and energy when when you know you'd get the same good food and service at a restaurant nearby.

Regardless how luxurious or lax the atmosphere is at a restaurant, I make sure I'm in my nicest clothes and best behavior. I treat the servers with the same kind of respect I'd give to politicians and royalty. In my eyes, people are the same. The only thing that sets us apart from each other is the way we present and conduct ourselves in public.

How you present yourself (with your attitude and appearance) instantly reveals your personality and upbringing. These are crucial qualities that need to be given much attention. The way you present yourself is also a representation of the kind of family where you came from. Personally, I hold my family's reputation to the highest degree.

Please allow me to share with you a short anecdote about my beloved grandfather.

I hope these few lines would give you a background of my giving importance to family values, pride and reputation.

My late grandfather, Manolo Mateo, was a retired police officer in Manila. He was a *mestizo* (of Spanish ancestry), like his father before him. My grandmother once told me that her father in-law was Caucasian-looking, with his alabaster skin, aquiline nose and generous height. My grandfather came from a family of police officers in Manila, one of his deceased uncles being a batch-mate at the academy and friend of the current mayor of the city, Alfredo Lim.

My grandfather passed away more than a decade ago from heart failure. In his lifetime as well as in our neighborhood, he was both feared and revered. His intelligence and clever mind were known to all townsfolk. I remember some of our neighbors, when having disputes and misunderstandings with one another, would stop by our house to seek counsel and advice.

At the time, I was living with my grandparents. My grandfather was the mediator and peacemaker. His decisions were deemed just and they were highly respected.

No one dared mess with my *yoyoy* (a Tagalog term of endearment I've become accustomed to in calling him due to my childhood stutter; it originates from *lolo,* meaning 'grandfather'). Despite the slight name change, my respect and reverence for him remained firm and unaltered. His approachable and charismatic personality, care and concern for the welfare of others, were his legacy. His authoritative stare spoke for itself—you simply had to obey or do the right thing without any question or rebuttal. His decision on matters and issues was always final, and every subject involved seemed satisfied with it. When he was angered by something or someone, his thunderous rage was heard several houses from ours. This, of course, seldom happened. One would always find him exercising his sense of humor or sitting in our front porch, chatting away with neighbors and relations alike—a typical pastime in the Philippines.

My *yoyoy* loved and adored my beautiful sisters—Mary, Angeli, Maria and Merryl—very much. While we were still in the Philippines, he made sure we lived comfortably, and that all of our needs were met. He and my grandmother, Norma, were our secondary providers—for food and sometimes, money—while Daddy was working abroad. I'm absolutely grateful for that and will never forget their acts of kindness and generosity.

I also believe it was from my grandfather that I inherited a strong sense of will and determination and perseverance; that no matter what hassles and obstacles stand my way, I'd deal with the issue head on.

Looking back, I remember that one spring day in 1999 when I stood in front of the mirror and vowed to change my looks, stressing and worrying a great deal. These days, my only worry is what shade to use on my hair next time.

I have come to terms with the average appearance of my outer exterior. I realize now that beauty truly lies in the eye of the beholder. I may look average to some, but alas, to others I know I am very beautiful and irresistible.

I believe as I grow older I think less and less of the barricades that stand in the way of my being content and confident with my looks. I simply move on and ignore those negative comments and other criticisms. As I sail through life, I learn how to be more kind to myself and more accepting of what I am, and thankful for what God had given me.

Speaking of giving, one has to be nice and generous to the valet employee, too. Just like when you would give a generous tip to the server at the restaurant when you liked the service, you should do the same to the valet boy. Yes, to park and retrieve your car is their basic job description, but to open its door and close it for you accompanied by a courteous and genuine smile? You simply have to do that justice.

I remember giving ten dollars to the valet person at the Downtown San Jose Marriott on one occasion. As I hopped in my Mercedes, the appreciative soul was nice and helpful enough to ask me if I needed directions. I thought he did a very good job. The reality is, you'll never know if you'll see him again or not—so make a lasting impression!

Exiting the hotel requires less artistry, but not entering. I always make sure I look poised and dignified, and also make eye contact with the staff at the front desk. If they beam a smile, I return the favor; if within two seconds there's none, I'd gladly initiate. One must remember that you are inside their establishment, and aside from the standard hotel rules, regulations and policies you're required to comply with, there is what I call a 'silent' form of courtesy. A sincere smile exudes friendliness and good intention, and it will earn you a good impression among the people you come across with.

Never look lost, confused or naïve in public places because people could be assessing you already, and you might look funny to them. One must always practice a look of confidence and class. Of course, such feat takes a lot of time and effort to accomplish, but once you get the hang of it, it boosts that self-confidence to sky-high proportions. You know right away no one could put you down or intimidate you because you're poised and in control of the situation.

Just like royalty, I always stand tall with my chin up and shoulders straight. I think it's my imposing height and posture that summon people's attention, and I must say I'm very proud of it. One advantage of being tall is that you command attention and respect among those around you. You just *can't* be ignored.

When you are inside a hotel and not sure of the way to the elevator, do not panic to the point that you run all over the place. Maintain your poise and grace, then glide slowly towards the front desk. Smile, greet the staff and politely ask any question you might have. One has to remember that not all women (even Hollywood celebrities) are blessed with these attributes. Do the best you can to exemplify this trait without looking like a try-hard.

I may not be a complete female in the most physical sense but I know for a fact that within me is a true, classy lady. I have received numerous compliments about the class and grace I exude. I remember one occasion many years ago while shopping with my then-boyfriend, Dave Mastersen, at a boutique in San Jose that caters to the clothing needs of transsexuals. The employee made a flattering remark when she said I was the "only customer with class" present at the store that very moment.

One thing I'm sure of when it comes to comparisons and contrasts with other transsexuals is that I know how to conduct myself when in public. I have manners and know how to practice proper etiquette. I have grace and class, and more importantly, I know very well how to communicate with people so that they'd feel at ease when in my presence.

Vanessa soars beautifully.

11

The Fabulous Experiences

Travel

Life is like going to a restaurant—sometimes it serves you well, sometimes it's really bad you just want to walk out from it. Good or bad, you still have to make a decision. I choose to accept both good and bad, live with it, but make see to it that I give myself a break, literally. Being a transsexual in this unpredictable world is complicated enough, so why make it even more complicated by worrying about the world's flaws, indifferences and imperfections? My solution is a well-deserved, rejuvenating vacation.

Our family trips and vacations are full of fun and new discoveries. Whether it's in Philadelphia or the Philippines, Mommy and I try our best to make such trips worthwhile.

San Diego is my most favorite destination. The beauty of Balboa Park, the cool breeze and quaint little shops in Coronado Island and trendy Downtown, all contribute to my unfaltering annual pilgrimage to this gorgeous city. In San Diego, I find peace and calm. It's my therapy.

Come April, during the spring break, Mommy and I would sojourn to Southern California. Our first stop: Disneyland—undoubtedly the "happiest place on earth." I can't speak for the rest, but in my case, there's not a single fiber in my body that doesn't become happy the minute I enter this enchanting kingdom.

Unlike other transsexuals, I am very comfortable being in the public eye even during daytime. In fact, I relish the freedom and carefree feeling it generates. I don't feel awkward at all. Just like a little child, I simply don't care about the prejudiced and critical eyes surrounding me, if there are some. I go on my business and it's a very fun experience; plus, of course, one must understand that *I* paid for my ticket to gain entry into that establishment, not them. I can do as I please and that is that.

Surely, every time I go to Disneyland, I become a little child again. I forget my problems and worries; fairy tales come true the minute I start to mingle with the

Princesses—Aurora, Cinderella, Belle and Snow White; and the excitement I feel is as intense as the Matterhorn and Space Mountain rides. The Disneyland experience is as irreplaceable as childhood itself. I don't want to leave. I don't want the fun to end.

I have no choice but to end it though, because it's time to drive farther south—to divine San Diego.

Friday is a favorite day of mine to drive to San Diego from Anaheim. Why Friday, I don't know. I just feel it's the perfect day for that. Maybe because there's nothing more perfect in my mind than a Friday luncheon at the Sheerwater Restaurant located inside the Hotel del Coronado. With its fantastic view of the Pacific Ocean and the mouth-watering dishes on the menu, a seat inside the Sheerwater is the best in town, at least within Coronado Island.

On some occasions, we would lunch out by the deck of the Hotel del Coronado where some of the best hamburgers are being served; not to mention the view once I take my seat: simply magnificent. There is nothing more soothing than the grand view of the Pacific Ocean, accompanied by its therapeutic breeze. The warm, clement weather found in San Diego reminds me of my native Philippines, without the humidity and extreme heat. San Diego is the best retreat for me. There's no place like it.

Mommy and I (and, on some occasions, my sisters too) have also made out-of-state trips in the past several years. In 2001 we visited Florida, the following year we went to New York and Las Vegas, and in June 2005 Mommy and I vacationed in the East Coast. We visited Maryland, Washington DC, Virginia and Pennsylvania.

The latter trip was a very enjoyable and educational experience. We visited the Capitol, Lincoln and Jefferson monuments, and other historic spots. It was a monumental feat for my 'womanhood' because for the first time, I really felt the chains of prejudice and discrimination off my wrists.

Standing in front of the Washington Monument, I felt a certain kind of indestructibility just like the gigantic stone near me; that in that very moment I was overly protected by one of the Founding Fathers of freedom. How ironic. It was overwhelming, too.

At the Pentagon Fashion Mall in Virginia, I saw for the first time a Swarovski store and became instantly bedazzled by one of the gorgeous crystal bracelets on display. I didn't hesitate buying it. It was a purchase that would continually harbor praise and compliments every time I wore it at parties and other special occasions. Friends and family members alike couldn't help but admire the beautiful craftsmanship and brilliance of the crystals themselves.

In Pennsylvania, Mommy and I visited Philadelphia and later drove all the way to Lancaster where the Amish community is found. It was a very unique experience, but the people were no different than every American I met in DC, Maryland and Virginia—nice, friendly and helpful. I remember this good-looking young guy who worked as a cashier for a convenient store at the boundary of the road that leads to the Amish community and his flirting ways; it made my trip even more memorable.

On the last day of our trip, we didn't waste a single opportunity to visit and appreciate one of the museums in D.C. where an Ella Fitzgerald exhibit was well underway. I am a lifelong Ella Fitzgerald fan. This particular exhibit had a special connection with me because of my admiration for Ella—her style of music, the versatility of her voice and her incomparable delivery. At home, I make sure I have my "Ella time" especially on weekends; listening to her numerous CDs while reading, writing, drawing or just laying down doing nothing.

Concerts and Other Musical Shows

Music is one of the greatest inspirations of my life. Seriously, without it, there'll be no sanity for me. My world would be dull and dreadful. Melodies and harmonies have touched, calmed and healed the human soul since time immemorial. No doubt, it had the same effects on me.

Nevertheless, music should be perfection. And perfection means Streisand, LaBelle, Khan, Houston, and Eder. The power and range in these artists' voices are stuff which my sanity is made of. It simply makes me realize my feet are still on the ground while their voices are four octave and up higher.

The incomparable vocals of Barbra Streisand, Mariah Carey and Linda Eder still reign supreme. Call me old fashioned but to me a song should be sung the traditional way: go by the original notes, no more, no less. No screaming, no shortcuts and no flaws. This is how my favorite divas do it.

The year 2006 was definitely a *divalicious* year for me. In October of that year, I got to see Mariah Carey perform in Oakland, and a month later, La Streisand graced San Jose. These events will go down in my personal history as some of the best experiences I had. Forever the memories will be etched on my mind.

Just like when going to the movies, I would only go if the movie itself suits my taste. I admit, I'm both critical and practical when it comes to the movies I am going to see; critical in the sense that I only watch those that make sense and practical because I want to get my money's worth.

It's no different when it comes to concerts and musical shows. You expect a great performance always. At a circus, would you rather pay for a crystal ball booth with a fake gypsy psychic inside, or watch a magician show his tricks? Of course, you would opt for the latter.

The year 1990 saw the advent of Mariah Carey. She was my number one favorite singer. Her voice was fresh, soulful and powerful. Not as powerful as Whitney's but hers had a more 'acrobatic' flair: fluctuating effortlessly from a lower range to a higher one, and vice versa. From her first hit song, *Vision of Love* to the most recent one, *We Belong Together*, she had my all out support. I grew up listening to her songs and relating to her lyrical sentiments.

So, when I heard on the radio sometime in the summer of 2006 that she'll be performing in Oakland, I immediately took my cash-stacked Louis Vuitton Speedy 30 out of my closet, plucked out a couple hundred dollars, and headed to the Ticketmaster branch at the San Antonio Shopping Center in Mountain View, California to buy tickets for me and Mommy. I simply couldn't afford to miss this event. I made sure I bought tickets ahead of time.

October 3rd was the big night and true enough, Mariah's show was larger than life. The Oakland Arena was packed, and the thunderous applause on Mimi's every performance was deafening. It was an impressive sight. The pop empress definitely achieved another crowning moment with the Bay Area crowd's support.

A month later, Barbra Streisand performed in San Jose. It was another main event I wouldn't miss for the world.

Streisand's major hits soared in the '70s—Mommy's teenage years. Therefore, it might be well considered to be in her era. But decades ago and up until the present, gays have had a special affiliation with Barbra and her songs. Gay men have embraced the Barbra phenomena, and the latter never failed to do them justice. I believe it's a relationship that will surpass all other relationships in terms of longevity. A couple of years ago, I began to feel the heat of the Barbra fever. It's never too late to become an adoring fan. After all, that's what legends are—they never surrender to time.

Now that I'm a full grown adult, I'm beginning to appreciate the music of Streisand even more, and relate to her songs with gusto. Her songs—particularly the Broadway produced ones—are fun, flirty and feisty. But the most important thing to me is how those songs are interpreted. Barbra's voice is an original masterpiece on its own—possessed only by one individual and impossible to be imitated.

Ignoring the sudden downpour while driving home that Monday night after the concert, I still had shivers up my spine. I never in my entire life imagined I would see Barbra perform live. It was a once-in-a-lifetime experience, and I absolutely reveled in the moment. I was proud to have had such experience.

But then again I am no stranger to concerts and musical shows. In August 2002, while vacationing in New York, Mommy and I, along with my three sisters, went to see the Broadway musical *Phantom of the Opera*. It was an experience beyond words. From the storyline to the singing, one couldn't help but be in awe. Such a genuine, riveting theme, and such great, timeless songs.

Also within the same month I saw Lani Misalucha—considered one of the most talented female vocalists in the Philippines—at the Nob Hill Masonic Center in San Francisco. Dubbed as 'Asia's Nightingale', this songbird is best known for her vocal prowess and range comparable to that of Whitney Houston. She's also credited to having a "million voices," with her unique skill in mimicking those of her counterparts in the Philippines, as well as some of those in the US, notably Britney Spears, Beyonce and Celine Dion. She now performs regularly in Las Vegas.

In February 2003, I visited the Philippines and part of my itinerary was to see Regine Velasquez—'Asia's Songbird'—in concert at the PICC (Philippine International Convention Center). She performed with world renowned pianist and composer, Michel Legrand. It was another fabulous experience for me; the highlight of my trip.

I'm a slave to music, I admit. I could also be a major critic. I prefer high, powerful voices because in my opinion, if you want to be called a "singer," you should be able to sing all kinds of notes—high or low—no matter what. No excuses. I only have ears and respect for the best and the greatest.

Regine's flawless four octave range beautifully resonated within the entire hall. It was mesmerizing. Song after song, one couldn't help but feel the perfection and power. Her beauty and grace only made the event more enchanting. Michel Legrand, noted for his collaborations with greats such as Sarah Vaughan and Barbra Streisand, were all smiles most of the time. He knew he made the right choice in the Philippines, if not, in Asia.

Gifts

In November 2003, during the Thanksgiving celebrations that year, my friend, Chris King, flew me to Los Angeles for a very relaxing weekend getaway. It was a gift from the heart. Days before Thanksgiving, I was involved in a car accident (I was not the one at fault) and upon learning that I had a very stressful time, my handsome friend flew me to L.A., picked me up in his sporty Miata at LAX, and ultimately took my stress away once back at his cozy abode near Downtown. I couldn't ask for more. For two days, all we did was drink, party and enjoy each other's company. Chris treated me like a princess. I'll never forget that. I never wanted to come back to the Bay Area afterwards. It was *that* great.

In August 2005, another handsome bachelor friend of mine showered me with all kinds of pleasures and presents. Patrick Larson of San Rafael, California is rich, handsome and single. But above all, he had a very generous heart. The very sexy lingerie and thong underwear from Victoria's Secret that he gave me are still boxed up and unused. That is how I treasure them.

I also would like to take this opportunity to thank a number of generous men who have offered me some of the finest and precious gifts a girl could receive. This is another reason why I feel a tremendous amount of pride in composing this autobiography. The men I met and dated are some of the best in the world. Because of their kindness and giving heart and the very special treatment they've bestowed on me, I'd like to thank them from the bottom of my heart.

My good friend, John Drissom, is probably the most outstanding in this category. The two thousand-dollar check he wrote me in 2006, the Nikon digital camera he gave me on my birthday that same year, and the Blackberry for my 30th birthday last May, are just some of the outstanding gifts I received from this masterpiece of a human being; proof that I'm simply one lucky girl to have met such a wonderful, kind-hearted person.

Reece Dobbs, part owner of a monthly publication in San Jose, is another friend of mine who never ceases to exercise his generosity towards me. The gold Anne Klein charm bracelet he gave me for Christmas 2005 is another piece of jewelry that I not only look to as another occupant of my jewelry box, but rather another treasure I hold close to my heart and memory. This particular trinket will forever remind me of Reece's kindness and down-to-earth nature despite his elevated rank in the social circuits of San Jose.

Dave Mastersen was a Porsche-riding guy I dated back in 2000. He was my first boyfriend. This wonderful person took me out lunching at some of the Bay Area's finest American, French and Indian restaurants; took me to the fabulous car shows in Palo Alto and wine festivals in Santa Cruz; and even examined great pieces of art inside the Triton Museum with me. He never showed any tinge of embarrassment or reservation from being seen in public with a transsexual. I really admire him and thank him for that.

From Dave, I received three of my most valued vintage dresses. They are rare in design and I simply adore them. He also took me shopping one time at a fetish store in San Jose wherein he purchased a gorgeous pair of platform shoes for me. They were so beautiful I had to put them on display in my glass curio cabinet.

He also gave many sacrifices just to be with me, to the point of risking his marriage. With that I will be forever humbled, and wherever he is now, I wish him the best, and I hope he and his wife have revived their happy married life since.

12

My Good Friends

Outstanding Friends

Who are we without having good, reliable and loyal friends? Without friends who show love and concern, we are nothing but lost souls. I'd rather be non-existent instead of being cursed for all my life for not having a purpose. To me, friendship is another vital part of our being. Friends are the secondary foundations of our lives next to family. Where family serves as the steel foundation rooted deep within, friends are the bricks and stones that keep us firm and indestructible.

I can't imagine living a life without friends and friendship. So while in this world, one of my important, personal missions is to keep the friendships I have with several individuals thriving and aglow. I make sure I keep regular communication with them, take time to celebrate significant gatherings and milestones, and more importantly, listen to their pains and problems when life is simply, well, just being life.

My girl friends Larissa, Abigail and Maude are always thankful for my presence at their never-ending parties and other family occasions. In turn, I am grateful for their invitation. They are like sisters to me. All my life I have believed that family comes first and these friends are considered family. I enjoy spending quality time with them whenever my busy schedule permits. The smile on their faces when they see me walk into their homes represent joy, fun and appreciation.

These people hold a very special place in my heart for they have always shown constant love and support over the years. The fact that they have witnessed my transition—from male to female—stood by me through it, and still embraced me as the same person and friend, is comparable to a heroic deed. I could never thank them enough.

Larissa Gesmundo is my *ate* (a Tagalog term of endearment for older sister). Though not a blood relative of mine, she is, after all, the best older sister one could ever have. Thoughtful, sincere and nurturing—these are her prominent qualities. I am so proud to have her in my life.

For ten years now, our friendship continues to blossom. She is always there to care, listen and show concern. She never missed any important occasion in my life, such as my birthday parties and other family gatherings. I love her with all my heart.

In August 1997, Pacific Bell hired me as a Telephone Operator, and during a lunch break from training, Larissa was the first employee to approach me and talk to me. Instantly, I felt good vibes from her and thought of her as a nice, friendly person.

I am very picky and discerning when it comes to choosing friends. Ninety-nine percent of the time, my instincts have served me right. I know right away if an individual is being sincere with me or just using me for convenience, such as money, favors and car rides. Larissa was none of those things. She was completely the opposite. What stood out the most upon our first meeting was her giving nature.

While taking one of my fifteen-minute breaks at work, Larissa handed me some Philippine-made pastry to eat. I will never forget that. Her generosity to close friends and family is matchless. I know this very well because from the first day I met her up until the present, I have been witness to this rare act of kindness. But, of course, it's an understatement. Larissa's kindness is inborn. What stands out the most is her giving heart. That's priceless!

Larissa has gone through a lot of trials and ordeals in life. What's amazing about this sister of mine is her perseverance and resolve. She faced her challenges with successful outcomes.

Despite the blows and lows she faced in her married years, Larissa never neglected our friendship. She was always there for me no matter what. Her tenacity was profound. Life and friendship went on.

I recall those late nights when we would hang around in the front porch of her Union City, California home, talking about life while smoking cigarettes, just enjoying a beautiful starlit night after a hearty dinner. Those were some of the priceless moments we shared. I really appreciated her openness and honesty. Through that I realized she trusted me. It meant a lot to me.

Larissa is an awesome cook. Her *kare kare* (a traditional Filipino dish made with ox tail and other meats, with some vegetables and peanut butter paste) was one of the best I ever had. I think the reason behind this is that she cooks from the heart and with enthusiasm. Larissa is both a perfectionist and a pleaser. Her friends' satisfaction in the dishes she prepares is one of her top priorities.

My *ate,* along with her two children, Devin and Cassandra, live a very comfortable and happy life, with fear in God and respect for others. I am so proud of them. I love them like my own family. It will never change.

Abigail Escalada is my *other* sister. In a recent party at her beautiful home in Mountain House, California, this very good friend of mine introduced me to her other guests as her "long lost sister." I'm so thankful we found each other because as the years progressed, I realized she had the genuine qualities of a real sister—caring, loving and always showing concern. I am so glad I met her and her wonderful family, because they have taken me into their clan as one of their own. Their smiling faces and warm embraces whenever we'd meet simply make me feel very lucky—lucky to be in the company of such beautiful, accepting people.

Abigail, like Larissa, was a coworker of mine at Pacific Bell back in 1997. Although in the beginning our relationship was not as close and binding compared to Larissa's, the friendship lingered and survived, and that's what matters.

Abigail and I were in very cordial terms. She made sure I was never forgotten on any of her or her relatives' special occasions and parties. With that, I felt a special kind of belonging. I realized that in them I found a new family as loving and caring as my own.

As the years went on, our friendship flourished even more. I attend almost every gathering the Escaladas and their relations host. There would also be strictly-family-affair-only gatherings that I feel so privileged to be a part of. This is a validation that Abigail and her family don't just look at me as another guest, but rather another family member. It means a great deal to me, and from the bottom of my heart, I thank them very much.

In my glass curio cabinet one would find the Sanrio items Abigail gave me back in May 1998—during my 21st birthday celebration—almost ten years ago. They serve as a constant reminder to the many years of good friendship I have with her.

A much older sister I'm proud to have is Maude of Santa Clara, California. A very good, reliable friend of mine since 1998, she has been with me through thick and thin, in good times and in bad. She had been witness to my imperfections and flaws, but still managed to look beyond and treat me as a good friend. She is perhaps the most loyal of all my friends.

The beginning of my friendship with Maude was surrounded by coincidental circumstances. One March afternoon in 1998, my friend Angie coaxed me into taking her coworker with us to San Francisco for a Saturday afternoon trip. The coworker was Maude. So, needless to say, I submitted to Angie's idea; taking into consideration the fact that it would be fun if we'd take along another person with us. I haven't met Maude previously, so I was excited to know what she was like. From the moment I met her until the time we parted ways later that evening, I never felt so much blessed.

I am so thankful to God for designing my fate with Maude. She is one of the nicest, most caring individuals one could ever meet. And when you become friends with her, you'd feel even more blessed. Her friendship is strong and sincere, and she keeps it in full bloom always with constant communication and thoughtful acts.

Maude is also the perfect hostess. Whenever I would come over to her apartment on a Wednesday or Friday night, she makes sure I'm comfortable and that I feel "at home."

Her pampering style is unrivaled. Back in 1998, during the first few months of our friendship and I'd come over to her house in Palo Alto, California, not only she would serve me the best breakfast, but the night before she would give me the most relaxing massage. It was so good I couldn't help but fall asleep (much to my embarrassment).

Maude's casa es su casa. I was always welcomed and accommodated well. Maude made sure I had good food to eat, had alcoholic drinks to enjoy, and had music for my pleasure; not to mention the dozens of DVD movies her brother, Noy, had for us at our disposal. I was never bored at Maude's place. Moreover, our friendship was never boring. There's always fun and excitement.

Maude is not only generous with kind, caring acts; she could also be generous with money and other gifts. Once when Maude won $1,200 from one of her favorite slot machines at the Cache Creek casino, I was surprised when she handed me $100 as a *balato* (a Tagalog term for winner's monetary gift to friends and relatives).

She also made sure our tummies were filled wherever we went. Whenever we'd go to Cache Creek, we'd try the sumptuous dishes listed on the menu of Kung Foo Fats, my favorite restaurant there.

On Christmases and birthdays, she would give her friends presents which she thinks are useful or would serve a purpose. The gray Old Navy fleece sweater she gave me years ago was one of my most favorite winter apparels; very warm and comfortable.

Maude would also do justice on my driving when it came to using my own car especially on our trips to Cache Creek: she would pay for the gas of my SUV back and forth. She made sure she took care of every single thing necessary in making our trip fun and worry-free.

A Friend Who Have Left Me, But Not My Heart

Getting to this part is a hard thing to do. But I simply have to, because in doing so, I am honoring the memory of a special person I have come to know, love and appreciate. Although she's not around anymore physically, in my heart and mind, she will always stay.

Tess Handa or *ate* Tess, as I called her with reverence when she was alive, was another sister I had who happened to live in Japan. She was the cousin of Larissa. Many years ago, she would visit the US to reunite and relax with her relatives. It was always a fun-filled trip and I'm proud to have been a part of some of those visits. Although married to a Japanese citizen, with two beautiful children, Tess made sure she hadn't forgotten her loved ones in America.

In the fall of 1998, we met for the first time. After my shift at work, I decided to stop by Larissa's house which was about ten minutes away from the Pacific Bell office. Tess always preferred staying at Larissa's house. She felt totally "at home" there. Larissa had intended to introduce me to her cousin whom she was very close to. The two weren't just cousins, but rather considered each other as sisters.

Within a few minutes of waiting in the living room, Tess emerged from her bedroom. We exchanged hugs and had a brief chat. It was getting late and I didn't want her to stay up any longer. I realized she had had a long trip and that she needed rest. The last thing I'd want is to become a pestiferous visitor, the kind who has no sense of time or consideration towards his or her host. To me, the important thing was I met Tess that night and got to know her a little bit even though our time was limited.

It was a meeting that would give way to a friendship which I vow to keep forever in my heart and mind, even though she's not around anymore. The impression she left and the kindness she had shown me are worthy of remembering her for a lifetime. It's as simple as that.

It's been more than three years since she passed away, but Tess will never be forgotten. She will always hold a special place in my heart because of her kindness, beauty and generosity.

Countless were the precious little things she had given me. I'm keeping them for good, and some are on display inside my glass cabinet. Tess knew I adored Sanrio characters, so she made sure I had some of its products: *Hello Kitty* and *My Melody* stationeries, pens, and other mementoes to name a few. To me, they are all fine little treasures that deserve to be kept and preserved.

During the 1998 and 1999 visits of Tess, we—Larissa and myself, along with Larissa's other relations who are also my friends, Marita and Cecille—made sure it was a worthwhile trip for our guest. We went out to town—clubbing, dining, partying and visiting scenic places in San Francisco. We simply had a blast.

Looking back at the pictures we took then, a feeling of pride and joy wraps my innermost senses—that even though she left us early, I'm glad I had the opportunity to meet her and participated in such activities that made her very happy while in America. It's the momentary happiness of the person you care about that matters most, and not uncertain things about tomorrow. One has to live for the day and simply enjoy it. We must always try to make the most out of each day because we don't know how long or short it will last.

The last time I saw Tess in person was in February 2003 during my Philippine visit. At the time, she had been undergoing various forms of treatment for cancer, but I was surprised and relieved to see her looking healthy and in good spirits.

God has been very good to her; he made sure she was in good condition during our meeting. I couldn't be thankful enough. If only I had some kind of healing power like God, I would cure her in an instant. But our one powerful God has his own reasons; reasons I dare not question.

We met at a popular restaurant and bar in Malate—the party hub of Manila. The place was called Ratsky's, a trendy, celebrity-owned party shack that provided good food and good music. Tess and I had a fabulous time. We danced, shared laughs, gossiped and talked about guys just like the good old days. Three of my aunts and a cousin also had the privilege to meet this wonderful friend. It was one of the happiest days of my life.

Her aura was happy and resigned. When I asked her if she would visit the US again, her response, accompanied by her classic pretty smile, was in the borderline of 'not sure' and 'no'. She also whispered in my ear that she found a new love interest and that she was very happy with the person. It was evident in her shy, girlish smile, and when the band onstage performed America's *All My Life*, she was giggling. It was all I wanted to know—that she was happy. To me, if my friend is truly happy with something or someone, I'm very happy for him or her, too. That's the most important thing.

13

My Favorite Things

Fraulein Maria's "These are a few of my favorite things" quote simply doesn't apply to me. I have a bunch of favorite things! Life is too short not to experience and possess wonderful things.

Mementoes and Souvenirs

My out-of-town trips would not be complete without me bringing home little things that would remind me of that particular place or event. For some odd reason, I feel it had been a part of my life, regardless how long or short my stay was. So, to make it more memorable, I take home with me a souvenir.

In 2004, during a Fourth of July family trip to Redding, California, on the special occasion of the Sun-Dial Bridge opening, I purchased a bracelet made with natural stones and crystals only found in, where else, Redding. The fusion of red, green and dark green gem stones and some crystals would forever remind me of the abundance of nature found in that place: lush green trees and exotic plants and flowers, the clear skies and the warm climate. It seemed as if those qualities culminated in the creation of that beautiful trinket. I can't wait for my return visit to Redding.

The following year, Mommy and I traveled to the East Coast, particularly the states of Maryland, Virginia, Washington D.C. and Pennsylvania. At the Pentagon Fashion Mall in Virginia, I chanced upon a Swarovski store and instantly fell in love with one of the crystal bracelets on display. I didn't hesitate buying it—tax-free. I knew I had great deal. I also realized I had a gorgeous choice because friends and family alike have constantly admired and complimented that particular piece of jewelry.

A few days later, during our sojourn to the Amish country in Lancaster, Pennsylvania, I made sure I didn't leave without taking with me something that would forever remind me of the innocence and simplicity of that place: a little Amish baby doll in a baby carriage. I bought it at a cottage-like souvenir shop along a major thoroughfare where both buggies and VW Bugs alike travel in peaceful co-existence.

Thousands of miles away from Pennsylvania, in beautiful San Diego, one would find me shopping at the quaint little shops along Coronado Island's famous Dock during my annual trip in the spring, examining a good number of accessories that I consider rare with enthusiasm. I never left the Dock empty-handed. It has become almost like a ritual for me—I simply *have* to shop there.

The pieces of jewelry and accessories I buy in San Diego are some of my most prized material possessions. They are very representative of myself, I believe: unique and always drawing attention. Due to the fact that they are extraordinary in terms of style and craftsmanship, I make see to it that I take care of them the best way possible.

Not all my souvenir collection and mementoes are made up of jewelry and accessories. Some also have relevance to the men I dated. They include beer and wine bottles, cigarettes and cigarette lighters, hotel soap and lotion, underwear and other small presents.

In my glass curio cabinet, one would find an armada of beer and wine bottles which constantly remind me of the fun I had with the men whom I shared those alcoholic treats with. Some might call it weird, cheap or crass, but I simply call it "fun." At least I know someone's really having a great time in this crazy, chaotic world we live in.

I praise health officials and other activists in their cause for anti-smoking policies, but I also believe that smoking after sex—especially the great sex I had—is very sexy. It might sound like I derived this notion from the dozens of Hollywood films with such scenes, but in reality, I enjoy doing it. The consequences are on me, so leave me be. In my glass curio cabinet, a mainstay would be a half-consumed Marlboro Lights cigarette pack along with a couple of lighters.

I also collect and keep hotel toiletries. I relish the idea of having "proof" that I've actually been to or stayed in that luxurious hotel, and, to top it all, had a fabulous time.

I could never guess the exact number of miniature lotion and shampoo bottles I brought home with me after a stay at these expensive hotels. One particular souvenir I value with much pride is the Bulgari bath soap I acquired from the Ritz-Carlton hotel in Half Moon Bay, California. At the Ritz-Carlton hotel, they treat you like a celebrity the minute you step out of your car up to the time the valet boy retrieves it; at least that was the case with me when I visited in December 2006.

My friend even suggested that I wore the classic white bathrobe so I'd have the "complete Ritz-Carlton experience." Indeed, it was one of the most comfortable and warm bathrobes I've ever worn.

Speaking of undergarments, I also have a penchant for asking some young men I date for their underwear, whether it's their boxers or briefs. There is a catch though. I only ask for the underwear of whoever is twenty-two years old at the time. For reasons I wouldn't bother explaining, I've always thought of twenty-two as the age when I would see him for the last time. Fate definitely assured me this. Brian, Carl and Trent were all twenty-two at the time when I last saw them.

In 2003, soon after my last meeting with Brian, I vowed to always ask for souvenir underwear from my younger companions. Surprisingly, most of the young bucks I captured obliged.

Books

Knowledge is priceless and so are some of the books in my possession. Some date back from early to mid-20th century. I'm proud to have them and I definitely have a wonderful time reading them. My passion for books and reading is never-ending. Learning for me is never-ending; it's a lifelong devotion.

'Read'—a classroom motto written on posters nailed to the wall, have left a most valuable impression. I remember almost every classroom in my high school had it. I'd like to take this brief opportunity to thank the teachers and other school officials out there for instilling that on the minds of their students. I personally considered it a form of self-fulfillment a long time ago. I've been an avid reader all my life. I vow to practice it for as long as my eyes and brain are functioning splendidly.

In my high school days in Mountain View, before the first period bell rang, one would find me at the library, reading Time or Newsweek, or any book about royalty. Not a minute wasted in school.

This is how I value learning—never be idle, never waste time. Feed your mind, whether it's with social, political or current events. The important thing is you are aware of what's going on around you and the whole world.

My thirst for knowledge could be traced back to that one poignant day in my childhood when I lost the Nursery Rhymes book set Mommy bought me. I forgot how I lost them, but never forgot each line of the popular rhymes and poems in there. From that moment on, I vowed to always take good care of my books.

Whenever I have time and not busy with work, I visit this low profile bookstore, Bookbuyers, in Downtown Mountain View. It's my favorite bookstore. It's also one of the favorite places I like going to when I'm in that area, seconded by the Kirin restaurant a couple of blocks away. Mountain View holds a special place in my heart because it's the first US city where my family and I settled.

Such is my loyalty to Mountain View that up to the present time, even though I live miles away from her, I wouldn't mind wasting gas and mileage just to visit, and continually relive that special feeling I had back in the fall of 1994, when I strolled along Downtown one October afternoon for the first time. I was instantly captivated.

Bookbuyers is a treasure trove for me. Each book is like a gemstone or a strand of gold—irresistible. The knowledge and information you'll acquire from that place are boundless. Every time I come there, the last thing I think of is leaving soon. I simply have to satisfy my eyes and feed my brain for hours.

The prices aren't bad either. In the summer of 2006, I purchased a used book about the Romanovs of Russia for less than twenty dollars. It was in "like new" condition, thick and overflowing with interesting facts and rare photographs of the long-gone era of this tumultuous dynasty. I feel so privileged to have it in my possession.

My interest in royalty is not limited to the Russian Imperial Family. The Windsors and their predecessors—the Saxe-Coburg-Gotha and Hanover lineages—are on top on my list. Never have I been so devoted in one particular royal family than that of Queen Victoria's. In my years of reading about her and her enormous family, I am proud to say I've memorized all the names of her children, children in-laws and grand-children, along with the dates of their births and deaths as well.

In my bookshelf one would find a number of books and other publications relating to Queen Victoria and her brood. At the present time, I am thumbing up the pages of a biography about his haemophiliac son, Leopold, Duke of Albany, father of Princess Alice Countess of Athlone, the queen's longest lived grand-child. She passed away in 1981 at the age of 98. I also have the late princess's autobiography, *For My Grandchildren*, which is considered a rare possession these days.

The very first purchase I made on a book about the British Royal Family took place in the Philippines, fourteen years ago—while I was a senior in high school. The book, entitled *Sovereign*, was about Queen Elizabeth II and her family. I deeply regret the fact that I failed to bring it along with me when my family and I migrated to the US in 1994.

Another purchase I made took place while I was a freshman in college at the Far Eastern University in Manila. It was a book about Prince Charles. Sadly, it had the same fate as that of Queen Elizabeth II's. Thinking about it regretfully, if only I could pull back the hands of time, they would be the first to find a spot in my US-bound luggage back in September 1994.

Being an avid fan of history, it's fair to say I also have quite a number of books related to this subject. Two of my favorites are *The Travels of Marco Polo* and *Heroes of European History*.

Good Food

Food to me is like choosing men—I only go for the best. I want nothing less. It has to satisfy my cravings and I will savor its very good taste.

There are only two great cooks I've come to know and given utmost respect to in the culinary field—my grandmother and Mommy. Grandma cooks the best traditional Philippine dishes like the *kare kare, menudo* and *dinuguan*; Mommy's specialties are spaghetti, *pakbet* (a traditional dish from the provinces in the northern region of the Philippines made with vegetables, pork and shrimps) and *torta* (ground beef mixed with beaten eggs then sautéed with bell peppers, diced onions, sliced carrots and garlic). Despite their different styles in cooking, one thing they have in common is making me fall in love with it.

Living with my well-to-do grandparents for several years, I grew up in a house where there was no shortage of food. My grandfather was a good eater, always requiring at least two kinds of dishes on the table on each meal. From him I inherited a passion for good food. Luckily for him, Grandma was a very good cook.

As I grew older, I also developed a connoisseur tongue. Personally, my grand-mother's cooking always set a standard. Any dish I had that didn't level with the taste and quality of her cooking was frowned upon.

Years later, I still set high standards, but this time, it was not about Grandma's cooking anymore, rather it was all about the dozens of American restaurants I've been to.

If I were to pay a good amount of money at a restaurant, they better serve me right and serve me with good food. It's one of my personal policies in life these days. I'm a very nice, considerate customer, but in return I expect the same treatment from the establishment that I go to. What best way to make my visit worthwhile and worthy of remembering than to serve me with delicious, good food.

Fifty percent of my social calendar is made up of dinner dates. My good friend, John Drissom, and I, would regularly dine out at these restaurants: the Thai restaurant Bhan Thai in Fremont; the Olive Garden in the same city, and the Mexican restaurant, El Burro, in nearby Newark. We always have the best experience and service at these places. Not only the food is good but the service as well. But nothing comes close to the level of service and sumptuousness of the dishes served than at Uncle Chong Chinese restaurant, also located in Fremont. The ambiance is very relaxed, the service very friendly and the owners make you feel as if you're dining at their home, not in a restaurant.

Even during my Pacific Bell days in the late '90s I've been dining out at Uncle Chong's.

Sometime in 1998, I had lunch there with my good friends Larissa and Abigail. It was also at Uncle Chong where I celebrated my 21st birthday that same year. The quality of food and service have not changed over the years—still exceptional.

Music and Dancing

When I'm not busy with work, one would find me organizing my enormous CD collection and listening simultaneously to some of my all-time favorites like Ella Fitzgerald, Sarah Vaughan, Natalie Cole and other legends whose singing greatness I have come to admire and appreciate.

Music is definitely a great inspiration for me. Love songs make me reminisce and dream of the few good men I have met and the fun times we've had; rock ballads electrify my senses, making me think and recall things well especially when I'm in a writing mood; and dance music is the wind that moves my body in the most wonderful and admirable way.

Ella Fitzgerald—the 'First Lady of Song'—is also first in my roster of all-time favorite female vocalists. She is the epitome of what a song and singing should be: never a wrong note, perfect in pitch and precise phrasing. Above all, her voice possessed a magical quality. She transcends a mere song into becoming the best rendition or interpretation you will ever hear. Some of my favorite Ella Fitzgerald renditions are *Misty, Over The Rainbow, The Lady Is a Tramp* and *Dancing in the Dark*.

Eartha Kitt is another favorite of mine. Although practically considered *way* too old for me to idolize, we're not too far apart in terms of wordliness and passion for men. Her song *Je Cherche un Homme* (I Want A Man) from the movie *To Wong Foo Thanks For Everything Julie Newmar* is perhaps my most favorite theme song for a movie. Her interpretation and delivery is as genuine as the French blue color. Above all, it strikes a chord in me: rich or poor, handsome or average-looking, it doesn't matter to me as long as my man loves me and makes me happy.

Linda Eder, though not widely known in the realms of popular music, is well appreciated and admired by me. Constantly compared to Barbra Streisand, I disagree. These two women have great, powerful voices, but Barbra is Barbra and Linda is Linda.

From the day I first heard her songs *From This Moment* and *After All* back in 1990, it never left my memory. Her voice is simply divine; high as the angels up in the sky, with a range and note-holding quality that are as everlasting as the universe. To some, this might be a common exaggeration from a die-hard fan, but I suggest you listen to her CDs first.

A New Life is one of my all-time favorite Linda Eder songs. One of the songs from the Broadway musical *Jekyll and Hyde*, this song has a special significance, personally.

It speaks of the 'what ifs' and alternate fantasies of life; that it would be a much better and happier life if all things went to our favor. But then again, life is not perfect. The only consolation I have is reveling in Linda's powerful delivery, especially the last few lines and her grasp on its last note: one of the longest I ever heard from a singer.

Personally, I have a collection of favorite songs that seem to have some relevance in my colorful life. These songs also serve as an inspiration in my day to day experiences. Some also make me reflect on past relationships and other affairs of the heart. Here are some of those songs that continue to ignite feelings of love, pride and triumph within me: Shirley Bassey's *Diamonds Are Forever, That's Life* and *This Is My Life*, Liza Minnelli's *The Look of Love*, Yvonne Elliman's *Moment By Moment*, Diana Ross' *It's My Turn* and *When You Tell Me That You Love Me*, Jennifer Holiday's *And I Am Telling You*, Patti LaBelle's *Over The Rainbow*, Chaka Khan's *Papillion* and *Through The Fire*, Sheena Easton's *Almost Over You*, Cyndi Lauper's *All Through The Night* and *My First Night Without You*, Whitney Houston's *I Know Him So Well* and *Run To You*, Natalie Cole's *Starting Over Again*, Swing Out Sister's *Precious Words*, Gloria Estefan's *Cuts Both Ways*, Heart's *All I Wanna Do Is Make Love To You*, Mariah Carey's *Without You*, Lisa Stansfield's *In All the Right Places*, Oasis' *Champagne Supernova*, Filter's *Take a Picture*, Aerosmith's *Crazy* and Depeche Mode's *Somebody*. Celine Dion's *Only One Road*.

I also enjoy the music of Tony Bennett and Michael Buble.

I'm proud to say one would never find me dancing the wrong way or with the wrong moves. I have received numerous praises and positive comments about how I took over the dance floor. In 2002, when my girl friends and I went to the club Q Café in Palo Alto, all eyes were on me. The DJ was playing Abba's *Danc-*

ing Queen; I glided gracefully to the dance floor with my partner, and ultimately left an impression among those who witnessed my art. "Guys stood there in awe with the way you danced, Vanessa," said my friend. "Including the bartender!" she added.

Dancing for me is another form of therapy. Whenever I dance, it's an open and carefree expression of my freedom. I am in total control. No one's telling me what to do or how to do things. I abide by no rules except mine, and I feel an overwhelming amount of power because I know I draw people's attention and ignite men's wildest imaginations. Whenever I dance, I know I am the center of attention, and that to me is another validation of how I effortlessly show the world what a unique and talented person I am.

Madonna is my number one dance icon. Her 1989 Video Music Awards performance of *Express Yourself* came as an epiphany. I admit, she was an instant inspiration. After that performance, I realized I will make dancing a part of my life, particulary during my high school years in the Philippines.

Many times I've been asked by my high school teachers in the Philippines to dance during school festivities and Christmas parties. Along with my two other gay friends, Jovette and Chun Chun, we would imitate dance performances of Madonna and Paula Abdul. Two of our most memorable performances were Madonna's *Vogue* during a Spelling Bee competition in 1990 and Paula Abdul's *Vibeology* during the 1992 Foundation Day celebration of my school.

Those were the halcyon days of my high school life in Manila. It was all about having fun, performing for classmates and teachers, and not really worrying about getting good grades. I had no regrets. My high school days in the Philippines are some of the happiest days of my life.

I also credit my weight loss to the art of dancing. In 2002, every day for two hours, I would play disco and J. Lo songs in our living room, and dance till I sweat buckets. Yvonne Elliman's *If I Can't Have You* and Donna Summer's *Last Dance* were among my favorite disco songs. From size 14, I got down to a mere size 9. At 5'10", my tall frame helped even more in projecting that slim image. Every one noticed it, and I was extremely proud of that accomplishment.

My forte in dancing lies within the Latin category. For some odd (and seemingly good) reason, I'm more attuned with its beat and rhythm. I always get praises and compliments with my sexy Latin moves. I always tell friends and family that my body was "made to dance." My Latin influences are none other than J.Lo and Shakira.

Also in 2002, at the height of the success of Shakira's number one hit *Whenever, Wherever*, the spotlight inside Molly McGee's in Downtown Mountain

View was specially beamed towards me, thanks to the DJ that Saturday night who played the aforementioned song. He surely noticed my great moves on the dance floor and made me the center of attention.

Keeping in Touch

Writing letters to relatives overseas is one of my favorite hobbies. I like knowing what's going on with their lives there, and likewise enjoy writing about my activities and other "gimmicks" here. Conversely, my relations seem to relish the entertaining and exciting stories I share with them.

My letters to them serve as a small window to my life here in America. In it I give them the opportunity to have a glimpse of Vanessa's life and lifestyle. When some of my friends here are sometimes too busy to listen, or simply not interested anymore because in the back of their minds they experience the same good things anyway, writing to my loved ones in the Philippines serves as a form of therapy. Those curious and interested relatives have a wide open ear for my exciting and revealing stories.

From the very beginning, my life to them has been an open book. I don't hide things or lie about things. The things I talk about are all products of what is essentially a much-vaunted life in America—the fun, the good life and the successes. Thankfully, my relatives are ever so enthusiastic in hearing them. I greatly appreciate their acknowledgement.

Ever since my family and I migrated to the US in 1994, I have kept in touch with almost all of my loved ones in the Philippines. They have been witness to my struggles and successes in this country. Through their letters they have sympathized, empathized and advised.

Ours had been a very special kind of correspondence, filled with care and concern. It was never a send-me-this-send-me-that type of communication. In fact, my relatives in the Philippines are some of the most humble, simple and sacrificing people one could ever meet. Whatever food they had on their table, they were content and thankful. Whatever money they had on their pocket, they made the most out of it. If I decided to send them financial help, that's because I wanted to, not because they asked me to. It always comes from my own decision, not theirs. They never imposed.

To make that correspondence even more special, they constantly offer me sound advice on many things—physical, spiritual and emotional. I could never thank all my aunts—Mari, Marnie, Martie, Emily and Yolanda—enough for the many times they've shown me love and concern through the dozens of advice they've offered. I treat their words golden. To have such wonderful aunts like them make me feel like the luckiest person on the planet.

Another regular preoccupation is the constant communication I have with my good friend, Bobby, who lives in New York. Bobby, who arrived in the States from the Philippines in the fall of 2006, had been one of those genuine, loyal and most trusted friends I could call. Our friendship dates back to 1993—when we were seniors in high school. In September the following year, my family and I moved to the US, and for twelve long years of separation, he had continuously kept in touch; sending me letters and greeting cards, further cementing our already strong and stable friendship.

These days, Bobby would call me once or twice every week, sharing new developments regarding his newfound life in America. I would reiterate to him that life here is completely different than that in the Philippines, and often times newcomers have to adjust and adapt. But Bobby is a very smart and hardworking individual. With a college degree on his belt and other accomplishments and recognitions, I'm sure it won't be long before he finds better career opportunities. More importantly, he has a willful heart. All I could advise him at this point is to have patience and perseverance. Eventually, he will survive and ultimately succeed.

These Days ...

In my free time, one would find me organizing my Hot Wheels toy car collection (I only collect its classic and "muscle" models), preserving and archiving old family pictures and exploring other artistic endeavors. I plan to write another book in the near future.

14

Remember Me Always

The first thirty years of my life were filled with many joys, men and boys; with happiness and openness; and love and love for life. Every morning when I wake up, the first thing I think of is my family, and the first words I utter are "Thank you, Lord, for another day." I know I've been blessed with a happy life. I simply don't dwell on the sorrows and failures. The tragedies I leave to Shakespeare.

Life is not fair—absolutely—but there are certain ways to overcome it. I have missed the wonderful opportunity of a college education, but that didn't make me dumb and stupid. Instead, I enriched my brain with knowledge, facts and other valuable food for the mind through endless reading and vigilance on the world's current events. My thirst for learning is simply unquenchable.

I had fallen in love with someone who didn't justify and acknowledge my feelings, but I managed to be stronger and put it behind me in the end. Instead of going insane, I channeled my devotion to the good, trustworthy people who have constantly stood by and supported me.

I became a victim of prejudice, discrimination and bigotry, but I managed to retaliate and come out victorious. Instead of letting it bring me down, I swam towards the surface and proved to the culprits that I am still here—a much stronger force to be reckoned with; unsinkable like the Titanic.

For every disappointment in life, there is success and jubilation in the end. We'll just have to learn to persevere and be patient always. It pays well in end.

Each day, I try my best to make it good and worthwhile. Each day, I live my life with zest and contentment. Each day, I try to make wonderful things happen. I'd want my friends and family to remember me this way. I might have not been the perfect friend, son, brother, cousin, lover, girlfriend, grandson, nephew or niece to you all, but I just want to let you know, in all those thirty years, all I did was try to please you and make you happy constantly. I just hope you will remember me always as the person who gave a lot, who have gone through a lot and sacrificed a lot, and whose concern for you will never diminish—for as long as there are thirty years constantly coming into my life. I love you and will continue to do so with all my heart.

Vanessa

About the Author

My name is **Vanessa Mateo.** I live in Milpitas, CA. I was born on May 17, 1977 in Manila, Philippines. I'm the eldest of six children. I am a female transsexual. My interests include reading, writing, fashion design, history and other subjects pertaining to various fields of study.

This autobiography has been a labor of love for me. I've devoted countless hours in writing this day and night, and exerted all kinds of effort to recollect and reproduce past experiences and memories which I think are all worthy of sharing to readers around the world. They will entertain and educate you. I hope my unique experiences in life would serve as an inspiration and lesson to most of you, especially those who are the same gender as me.

978-0-595-44624-7
0-595-44624-8

www.ingramcontent.com/pod-product-compliance
Lightning Source LLC
Chambersburg PA
CBHW051438280526
45785CB00003B/1333